Wales Co...
Tenby to...

Chris Moss moved to Laugharne in
Carmarthenshire in March 2012 to escape
London and do some writing. Born in
Lancashire, he spent ten years after university in
Buenos Aires as a teacher and journalist and later
worked for the *Daily Telegraph*, *Time Out London*
and *BBC History Magazine*. He has edited and written
guidebooks to ...
author of a cu...
book is a nove...

Wales Coast Path

Tenby to Swansea

Chris Moss

Aurum

First published 2013
by Aurum Press Limited
74–77 White Lion Street, London N1 9PF
www.aurumpress.co.uk

Book design by Robert Updegraff
Printed in China

Cover photograph: *Three Cliffs Bay, Gower Peninsula*
Half-title photograph: *The Wales Coast Path near Marros Sands*
Title page photograph: *Brandy Cove*

Aurum Press want to ensure that these National Trail Guides are always as up to date as
possible – but stiles collapse, pubs close and bus services change all the time. If, on
walking this path, you discover any important changes that future walkers need to be
aware of, do let us know. Either email us on **trailguides@aurumpress.co.uk** with your
comments, or, if you take the trouble to drop us a line to:

Trail Guides, Aurum Press, 74–77 White Lion Street, London N1 9PF,

we'll send you a free guide of your choice as thanks.

Contents

How to use this guide

This guide to the 129.2-mile (208-kilometre) Tenby–Swansea section of the Wales Coast Path is in three parts:

• The introduction, with an historical background to the area and advice for walkers.

• The Coast Path itself, split into twelve chapters, with maps opposite the description for each route section. The distances noted at the start of each chapter represent the total walking length of that section. There may be some variation, depending on whether firing ranges are open or if you head off to a recommended side-walk, such as at Worm's Head on the Gower. An estimate of the total ascent for that section is given, along with the altitude of the highest point you will encounter that day. This part of the guide also includes information on places of interest as well as a number of short walks which can be taken around each part of the path. Key sites are numbered (**1**, **2**, **3**, etc.) both in the text and on the maps to make it easier to follow the route description.

• The last part offers useful information, such as local transport, accommodation and organisations involved with the relevant section of the Wales Coast Path.

The maps have been prepared by the Ordnance Survey® for this Trail Guide using 1:25 000 Explorer™ maps as a base. The line of the Wales Coast Path is shown in yellow, with the status of each section of the trail – footpath or bridleway, for example – shown in green underneath (see key on inside front cover). These rights-of-way markings also indicate the precise alignment of the Wales Coast Path, which walkers should follow. In some cases, the yellow line on these maps may show a route that is different from that shown on older maps; walkers are recommended to follow the yellow route in this guide, which will be the route that is waymarked with the distinctive dragon-shell symbol 𝔤 used on the entire Wales Coast Path. Any parts of the path that may be difficult or confusing to follow on the ground are clearly highlighted in the route description, and important points to watch for are marked with letters (**A**, **B**, **C**, etc.) in each chapter, both in the text and on the maps. Some maps start on a right-hand page and continue on the left-hand page – black arrows (➡) at the edge of the maps indicate the start point.

Should there be a need to divert the Wales Coast Path from the route shown in this guide, for maintenance work or because the route has had to be changed, walkers are advised to follow any waymarks or signs along the path. Also, there are a few sections where a low-tide option is given; do not try to use high-tide routes if the tide is coming in or is already sufficiently high to block your path.

Distance checklist

This list will assist you in calculating the distances between your rest stops and proposed overnight accommodation and in checking your progress along the walk.

Location	Approx. miles		Approx. kilometres	
	from previous point	from Tenby	from previous point	from Tenby
Tenby	0	0	0	0
Saundersfoot	4.1	4.1	6.6	6.6
Wiseman's Bridge	1.3	5.4	2.1	8.7
Amroth	1.9.7	7.3	3.1	11.8
Marros	2.2	9.5	3.5	15.3
Pendine	2.9	12.4	4.6	19.9
Laugharne	5.8	18.2	9.3	29.2
Lower St Clears	4.9	23.1	7.9	37.1
Llansteffan	9.7	32.8	15.6	52.7
Carmarthen	9.2	42.0	14.8	67.5
Ferryside	8.7	50.7	13.9	81.4
Kidwelly	5.3	56.0	8.5	89.9
Pembrey Forest	4.6	60.6	7.5	97.4
Burry Port	4.5	65.1	7.3	104.7
Llanelli	4.1	69.2	6.6	111.3
National Wetland Centre	4.0	73.2	6.4	117.7
Gowerton	4.7	77.9	7.5	125.2
Pen-clawdd	2.7	80.6	4.3	129.5
Llanrhidian	4.9	85.5	7.9	137.4
Landimore	2.3	87.8	3.7	141.1
Whiteford National Nature Reserve	2.2	90.0	3.5	144.6
Spaniard Rocks via Whiteford Point*	6.2	96.2	10.0	154.6
Hillend	1.4	97.6	2.3	156.9
Rhossili	2.2	99.8	3.6	160.5
Port Eynon	7.1	106.9	11.4	171.9
Oxwich	4.5	111.4	7.3	179.2
Three Cliffs Bay	3.6	115.0	5.8	185.0
Caswell Bay	5.1	120.1	8.3	193.3
Mumbles	3.2	123.3	5.2	198.5
Swansea	5.9	129.2	9.5	208.0
* Spaniard Rocks via Bone Cave	3.6		5.8	
Rhossili to Worm's Head and back (off the main WCP)	4.4		7.1	

Key map

Wales Coast Path – Tenby to Swansea

1 Chapter start point

0 km   5

0 miles   5

The cast-iron lighthouse at Whiteford Point, built in 1865.

PART ONE
Introduction

Introducing the Wales Coast Path

The Wales Coast Path (WCP) – or, in Welsh, Llwybr Arfordir Cymru – opened on 5 May 2012. Waymarked by a distinctive blue-and-yellow dragon-shell symbol, it runs for 870 miles (1,400 km) from Queensferry on the River Dee, not far from Chester, to Chepstow on the River Wye. Along the way, it passes through the popular resort towns of north Wales, around the Isle of Anglesey and the Llŷn Peninsula (an Area of Outstanding Natural Beauty), along Cardigan Bay and then follows the established Pembrokeshire Coast Path (a National Trail).

After Amroth it enters Carmarthenshire, zigzags around that county's three estuaries and sweeps around the Loughor to go around the Gower Peninsula all the way to Swansea – the last stretch, from Tenby to Swansea, provides the focus of this book. After Swansea, the path heads for Neath and Cardiff and the heavily populated stretch of coast of the Severn Estuary.

While most trails and footpaths are there to get those who enjoy walking as a pastime away from built-up areas, the WCP is clearly a more varied affair, passing through industrial and post-industrial areas as well as dozens of conurbations. The path is a site of leisure and pleasure, but it is also a statement of national pride, bringing Wales together in one single symbolic coastal loop.

The other motives for the path are obvious. With the post-war decline of coal mining and heavy industry, Wales has looked to tourism to rebalance its economy. The success of the Pembrokeshire Coast Path, which opened in 1970, provided plenty of evidence that tourists from the UK and beyond are drawn to the rugged Welsh coast and that walkers in particular are not deterred by the weather. By promoting the WCP as the world's only all-country coast path, Visit Wales has already garnered plenty of media attention. The Welsh government says it expects the footpath to draw an extra 100,000 visitors to Wales every year.

The WCP project was born in 2006. While Pembrokeshire, Gower, the Llŷn Peninsula and Ceredigion already had coastal paths – or paths under development – the new sections required some hefty funding to build paths and install fences, gates, stiles and waymarkers. The money came mainly from the Welsh government and local authorities (£12 million to 2013), with an additional £4 million from the European Regional Development Fund. The challenges facing the Countryside Council for Wales – the body responsible, till March 2013, for delivering the WCP – were not insignificant. With much of the land on the coast owned by farmers and other private landowners, the route had to take into account the views of individuals and communities across sixteen local authorities, as well as the regulations governing the land it passes through – including two National Parks, eleven National Nature Reserves and many Wildlife Trust, RSPB and National Trust estates.

Neither is it without its challenges for walkers. Major estuaries – such as the three-pronged estuary around the Llansteffan Peninsula in this guide – mean the path has to drive deep inland for long sections. Where possible, the path-builders have sought to make the walk as pleasant as feasible, even when the coast is miles away: where the path rises high there are some striking views of castles, islands, estuaries, hills and mountains, and away from the coast are the bars, restaurants and hotels that make a walking holiday a pleasure as well as a worthy endeavour.

Not all the farmers raising stock and cultivating crops along Wales's coast have moved their herds or created space for the path to pass through. At times, the land is sodden or downright boggy, the bullocks are frisky and the signage is not the clearest. Where there's MoD land or where the path follows a roadside to keep off a farmer's field, the walk is less than bucolic: from Pendine, for instance, you have to follow a fenced-in corridor for hundreds of metres. As the years pass, the path will mature, habits will change and walkers will become common sights on the WCP. It is hoped the infrastructure will be finessed too.

Only a handful of people will walk the entire length of the Wales Coast Path. David Quarrell, who set off to walk it on the opening day, completed his journey – adding on a further 177 miles (285 km) by including the Offa's Dyke National Trail – in 72 days (plus 10 days' resting). Anne-Marie Beresford-Webb ran the same route in 41 days. For most of us, the WCP will be enjoyed as a week-long or two-week holiday, or over a series of weekend walks. It is one of the most varied footpaths in Europe,

passing through resort towns, along cliffs, along river banks, across beaches and past pristine marshes and sand dunes. A fascinating interface between land and sea, it is also a backdrop for history and culture and if it is, by definition, at the geographical margins of the nation, a walk along it is, in its way, the quickest route to the heart of the land and its people.

The Welsh: a coastal people

If the popular image of Wales is of green valleys and moody mountains, it could equally be argued that it is a country of coast and river, estuary and headland. The two biggest cities, Cardiff and Swansea, are on the sea, and many other major towns and villages – some of which were once far bigger than they are now – have evolved around inlets and ports. Climate and geography are the underlying reasons for this – the weather is milder on the coast and it was once much easier to travel by sea than over land – and these factors led in turn to trade hubs all along the coast. In

Three hogsback-style graves at St Michael's Church, Llanfihangel-abercowyn.

Saundersfoot harbour.

this guide, from the coal around Amroth to the cockles at Llansteffan to the metalworks at Llanelli, the coast has defined the evolution of the people and places of south-west Wales.

Though many of the places through which the Tenby–Swansea section of the WCP passes have Welsh as well as English names (Laugharne/Talacharn, Ferryside/Glan y Fferi), you won't necessarily hear a lot of Welsh spoken during your walk. The 'Landsker line' is the term used to describe the language boundary between Welsh-speaking and English-speaking Wales, and the Carmarthenshire coast, like the south Pembrokeshire coast, has been, historically at least, predominantly English-speaking. A chain of castles was built along the edge of the southern slopes by Norman invaders between the 12th and 14th centuries to keep the natives at bay and to deter any potential new invaders. Some of these are now skeletal ruins, but at Kidwelly the castle is intact and imposing and a powerful reminder of the military and strategic importance of the coast.

In the 12th century, Pope Calixtus II decreed that two pilgrimages to St David's were equivalent to one to Rome ('*Roma semel quantum dat bis Menevia tantum*'). But pilgrims following the southern coast of Wales did not, for all their faith and fervour, have to tackle a coast path. Instead they waded through the shallow watercourses and, when necessary, used rafts or boats to get across the estuaries. Many of these services lasted till modern times and all along the coast you will see the names of towns and landmarks like Ferryside, Ferry Point and Old Ferry. Sadly, the only safe crossing these days is to go round – mudflats, sandbanks and fast tides can trick even the locals.

In industrial times, the coast provided the fastest means of getting the coal, or iron, or timber, or tin to market. While some former ports are now mere ghosts of what they were in the past – you will struggle to imagine tall ships docking at St Clears and Loughor, or Laugharne heaving with hundreds of fishermen and merchants – there are vestiges of industry at Llanelli and around Swansea harbour. But over the last two centuries first the railway and then the roads moved power and commerce inland and the coast has been re-invented as a leisure space for sun-lovers, swimmers and watersports enthusiasts – and now for walkers.

Tenby to Swansea

The rationale for this book is simple. The Pembrokeshire Coast Path, established in 1970, runs for 186 miles (299 km) from St Dogmaels to Amroth. It's a beautiful, deservedly popular National Trail through a stretch of coastline almost entirely designated as National Park, taking in high limestone cliffs, sandstone coves, estuaries and sandy beaches.

This guide picks up the baton from Tenby (a pleasant town and an easy place to get to by public transport) and follows the coast eastwards. While not all of the subsequent coast is quite as picturesque as Pembrokeshire's, there is logic in linking the two sections. For one, keen walkers can do a continuous 315-mile (507-km) walk. Secondly, there is a geographical and cultural continuity: south Pembrokeshire and south Carmarthenshire are below the Landsker line, sharing the same Norman and English heritage, and historically linked through maritime trading and industry.

But walking from Tenby to Swansea needs no justification beyond the sheer pleasure of being in some of Wales's most varied coastal topography. If there is one word to describe the first half of the walk covered in the guide it is 'estuarine'. The three estuaries that have formed around the Llansteffan Peninsula – the Tâf, the Towy (Tywi),

and the Gwendraeth – dominate the landscape as they do much of the walking. All the rivers served south Wales as vital communication routes long before roads were built, and all contribute to the geography of salt marshes and sandbanks, pills (drainage ditches) and ports, beaches and burrows (dunes), cliffs and canals.

The guide outlines the walk west to east, to provide continuity with Aurum Press's guide to the Pembrokeshire Coast Path and to give visitors the best chance of enjoying the walk with the wind and rain behind them. If the coast between Amroth amd Swansea is not a continuously harmonious or pretty landscape, it has other virtues. Carmarthenshire is south Wales's undiscovered county, and as soon as you leave Amroth you will come across fewer people, less tourist tack, fewer caravan sites and, indeed, fewer walkers. The castle towns of Laugharne, Llansteffan and Kidwelly, and the county town of Carmarthen – all of which came to prominence during the Norman era – are of some historical interest. Names will crop up time and again as you walk, including historical figures such as Owain Glyndŵr, the last Welshman to be Prince of Wales and a fierce opponent of the English usurpers, and Sir John Perrot, a local landowner said to have been the illegitimate son of Henry VIII, who served as MP for Carmarthenshire but was later tried for treason and died in the Tower of London in 1592. He is memorialized at Sir John's Hill (see box, page 44) and his former residence near Llansteffan is still standing (at Trefenty Farm).

Dylan Thomas's legacy is like a long poem along the coast, from Cwmdonkin

Drive in Swansea, where he was born, to Fern Hill near Llangain, where he spent his childhood holidays, to Laugharne, where he is buried – see boxes, pages 43 and 128. You may also come across Merlin and King Arthur, the fire-breathing Wyrm and the Verry-Volk – all have spent time along the coast here (probably).

Less poetically, from south Pembrokeshire to Pembrey, the MoD tests everything from small arms to missiles to fighter planes and, as you will see from the OS maps, there is a series of Danger Areas right along the coast. Since the Second World War, the remote dunes, marshes and beaches of south-west Wales have been considered a relatively unpopulated, out-of-the-way place for sensitive military tests and on weekdays you may well find your peace shattered by the screaming engines of a jet as it banks over Carmarthen Bay. Fortunately, at weekends most of the testing and flying stops and the guide has suggestions for routes to use, or avoid, depending on the circumstances.

As you forge east you come to the contrasting delights of post-industrial Wales (especially at Llanelli and Swansea) and the Gower Peninsula, which was the first area in Britain to be designated as an Area of Outstanding Natural Beauty, back in 1956. Llanelli is no longer the Tinopolis it was during the late 19th century, and the coast here has been cleaned up and regenerated with parks and a 13.7-mile (22-km)-long coast path for walkers and cyclists. Swansea, the coda to the guide, is still, to quote Dylan Thomas an 'ugly, lovely town', but after days and nights spent on the lonely rural edges of Carmarthenshire, you will welcome the food and drink, arts and culture of Wales's second biggest city.

Planning your walk and accommodation

The 129.2 miles (208 km) between Tenby and Swansea can be completed inside a week if you are fit and keen. Two weeks would give you more chance to linger and enjoy the castles, beaches, food and drink and other attractions along the way. There is accommodation at many points along the path, from caravan sites and chalets at Pendine and Pembrey to boutique hotels in Laugharne and Mumbles. There are B&Bs in the smaller villages, so you can choose to break your journey according to your pace and pleasure.

You can, of course, approach the WCP in short sections, perhaps visiting over several weekends. This way you will see it in a range of seasons and under different weather conditions and tides, adding to the richness of your experience of the coast.

Whatever your approach, try to book transport and accommodation well in advance, especially in summer. Swansea and the Gower are easily accessed using rail or road transport. For further information, see page 137.

Carmarthenshire, it has to be said, does not have the best public transport links, and the coast, in particular, is a good way from the main West Wales railway line. For information about buses, see page 137.

The WCP is intended for walkers, not horseriders or cyclists. There are stiles and kissing-gates in all sections of this guide, and there are steep hills and cliff edges, making anything except walking and jogging dangerous. Note also that

Three Cliffs Bay.

there are long sections of the path that take you away from inhabited areas and roads; these areas are easily identifiable on the OS maps in this book.

Make sure you have snacks and drinks on the WCP; some sections offer very little in the way of refreshments and in rural Carmarthenshire opening times can be short and unpredictable, especially in winter. There are some benches, but you may have to sit on the ground to rest and/or eat, so take a waterproof blanket or a cagoule you don't mind sitting on.

Wear good boots and take walking poles if you need support on steep climbs and/or descents. If walking in winter, take a torch, and always carry warm clothes, waterproofs and a hat and gloves. West Wales is always appearing on the weather forecast because it is changeable and a rain squall can blow in at any time of the year.

Keep dogs under control at all time and if you are walking with children take special care walking on cliffs and near the many marshes along this route.

If you have mobility issues or are in a wheelchair, many sections of the WCP are problematic, but the 12-mile (19.3-km) section within the Millennium Coastal Park between Burry Port and the Discovery Centre in Llanelli is paved and basically flat, making it ideal for wheelchairs, prams and bicycles. Contact the Countryside Council for Wales for more details; see page 136.

Do not attempt the walks unless you are fit enough to complete the section, and if you have any issues with walking or fitness, check on the emergency services available and the back-up provided by your insurance company.

Safety precautions

The most likely hazards on the WCP are sprains and strains caused by uneven ground or slipping while crossing stiles. But keep an eye on the weather forecast and, in particular, the rain, as the ground can become horribly sodden. There are high sections, especially just after Amroth, near Llansteffan and along south Gower, and you should take special care here to avoid walking close to the cliff edge.

Do not take shortcuts by attempting to cross the estuaries. The tides here are fast and the tidal range is high, especially at spring tides (the high tides that fall twice a month, on new and full moons). You may see local anglers doing precisely this, but the sandbanks and mudflats hidden at high tide and exposed at low tide are extremely treacherous. Similarly, try to stay off the marshes of north Gower and near Laugharne as they can also become dangerously spongy. Check www.tidetimes.org.uk for tide tables. The most useful tables will be those for Tenby, Ferryside, Burry Port (for Whiteford Point and north Gower) and Mumbles (for south Gower).

Three highlights of the walk

Saundersfoot to Pendine

This early section takes you from the pretty coastal town of Saundersfoot, through old railway tunnels, past a great pub with a sea view at Wiseman's Bridge and then up to the cliffs above Marros Sands, concluding with a splendid view of Pendine Sands.

Pembrey Burrows and Saltings

There are many low-lying coastal systems during the course of this walk, but there's something especially dramatic about walking out of Pembrey Forest into this short stretch of salt marsh and dune. Look out for orchids and dune pansies, plovers and skylarks.

Whiteford Point to Worm's Head

The whole Gower is wonderful, but this walk around the western edges takes you from the mudflats and sandbanks of the Loughor Estuary to a lovely, ruinous old lighthouse, past great beaches and out to the wild, wind-blasted promontory of Worm's Head.

Worm's Head seen from Rhossili.

Old railway tunnel near Saundersfoot.

Sand dunes near Pembrey.

Mumbles Head – some historians believe that Swansea was originally founded on this lighthouse island.

PART TWO
Wales Coast Path
Tenby to Swansea

Tenby (Dinbych-y-pysgod) to Amroth

passing Saundersfoot and Wiseman's Bridge

7.3 miles (11.8km)

Ascent 1,542 feet (470 metres)
Highest point 289 feet (88 metres)

This first stretch is a good introduction to the Welsh coast, with quite a few ups and downs and some highish walks through woodland and along the tops of cliffs – and one long, steep set of steps to warm up those leg muscles. In summer there are a few small beaches that might tempt you to take a dip, as well as some good picnic spots along the way.

Both Tenby and Saundersfoot are well served by daily bus and rail services from Swansea and Cardiff. However, should you wish to use Saundersfoot railway station, note that it's 2 miles (3.2 km) inland of the village and the coast path.

Look out for… Tenby's walled Old Town, St Catherine's Island, Lady Cave Anticline, railway tunnels near Saundersfoot, Wiseman's Bridge Inn

Before you leave Tenby, take a look around. The Old Town **1** is tightly constrained within its medieval walls. Parts of the walls are in good repair, although their presence does create traffic problems, and the rather tacky seaside resort shops don't exactly complement the backdrop.

The huge South Gate has been knocked about a bit over the years in order to allow traffic to pass through it; the resultant Five Arches form the town's worst bottleneck. The ruins of the castle can be seen on Castle Hill, which also supports the town's excellent little museum. Other ancient buildings include St Mary's Church, the largest medieval parish church in Wales; the Tudor Merchant's House; and the little

fisherman's chapel close to the harbour. In Tudor and Stuart times Tenby was an important fishing and trading centre, and there were many powerful merchants in the town. Later the town became a popular health resort.

St Catherine's Island has a Victorian fort, built in 1868–75 to provide an 'early warning' defence for the Milford Haven waterway. Just above Castle Beach you can see the earliest lifeboat station, abandoned because of launching issues. On the north side of Castle Hill, between the gas lamp standards, are the steps that led to the old Victorian Pier built in 1897. A little further along is the new (third) lifeboat station, not far from the second one.

The harbour **2** is a hive of activity when the tide is in. If you are staying a couple of days you may wish to catch a boat over to Caldey Island, owned by Cistercian monks, who keep a monastery here – visits are allowed between Easter and the end of October.

Resume your walk at the harbour and follow the Promenade northwards along North Beach, ascending to the cliff top via one of the flights of steps. Then follow The Croft northwards and continue along the road. The route now takes you inland. There are National Trail acorn waymarks on lampposts, leading you north until you reach the coast path proper.

The Tudor Merchant's House, Tenby.

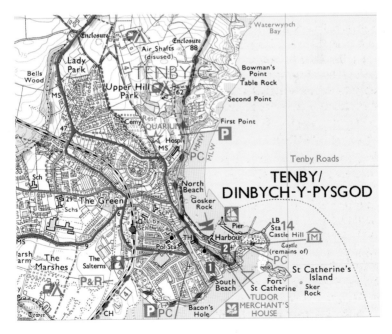

At Waterwynch, a pleasant wooded valley dominated by a view of a large caravan park to the west, turn right if you want to visit the beach. Alternatively, follow the National Trail fingerposts through the larch woodland **A**; you will eventually regain contact with the coast. Continue through attractive sheltered clifftop scenery until you reach Lodge Valley, which is thickly wooded with larch and pine. The climb northwards out of the valley is very steep **B**.

At Monkstone Point there are a number of paths to choose from, but views are somewhat restricted by the coniferous woodland. One path leads out to the headland and provides the best views. A footpath with over a hundred steps descends to the firm sands of Monkstone Beach, but stick to the path and do not try to scramble down the unstable slopes **C**. Once down at beach level, you can scramble across the headland col and (tide permitting) walk on the beach all the way to Saundersfoot. This route can be recommended only to those who are familiar with the tides in the area. If the tide permits, you can even continue all the way to Amroth on the sand.

The Coast Path between Monkstone Point and Saundersfoot provides a pleasant walk, mostly through clifftop woodlands. Sometimes it is precariously close to the cliff edge, which is hidden by vegetation in places, so be careful. Because the south-westerlies are blowing across land there is no damage to the trees here from salt spray, and these ancient coastal woodlands are among the most sheltered to be seen on the trail.

There is access to Saundersfoot beach beside the stream **D**. If the tide is high, take The Glen road, join the B4316 and follow it through to Saundersfoot. If you descend to the beach, detour a little way to the south to see the famous Lady Cave Anticline (a tight fold in the Coal Measures) before walking north towards the harbour.

Saundersfoot Harbour **3** was built largely for the coal-exporting trade. The village was insignificant until the 1800s, with most of the locally mined coal being exported from the beach. But then the growing demand for Pembrokeshire anthracite led to calls for a proper harbour, and building was commenced in 1829. Many of the local collieries were connected to the harbour by narrow-gauge railway tracks that ran through the village. One of these followed the coast via The Strand (note the parallel black lines in the asphalt commemorating this fact) and through three railway tunnels en route to Wiseman's Bridge and Stepaside. This is the route followed by the coast path. The third tunnel, the longest, is low-ceilinged and very dark, so walk with care.

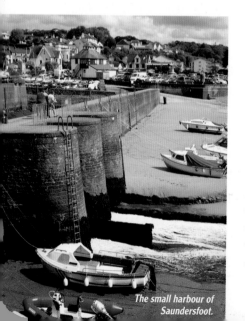

The small harbour of Saundersfoot.

North of Coppet Hall Point the path follows the old railway track. The cliffs above it are notoriously unstable, with ironstones exposed in the Coal Measures. If this route is closed because of rockfalls, it is possible to follow an alternative path along the cliff top **E**. At low tide, some walkers familiar with the tides choose to walk on the beach from Saundersfoot Harbour to Wiseman's Bridge.

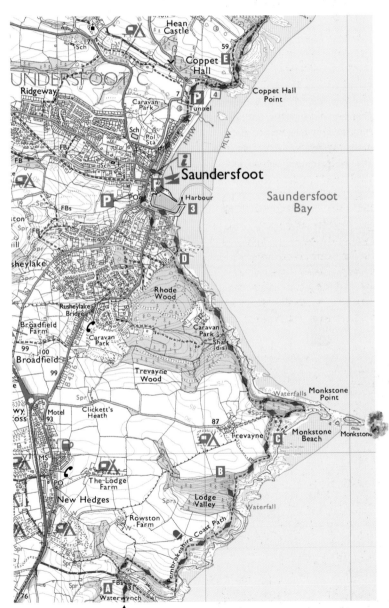

Pleasant Valley **4**, which runs inland towards Stepaside, was a centre of industry in the 19th century.

Follow the road past the Wiseman's Bridge Inn – an ideal stop for an al fresco pint and snack, weather permitting – then climb the hill and bear right. Eventually the road comes to an end and the path follows a bridleway that has been surfaced as part of the Celtic Cycleway. The path/cycleway now runs some way inland. As you approach Amroth turn right off the track **F** and cross the field (a nice picnic spot), passing into a little patch of woodland and then descending into the village.

The final half-mile or so of your walk is on the road. Amroth **5** is a straggling village, which was originally a small miners' settlement. On the seaward side of the road are the storm-beach and coastal defences; the village wages constant war with the sea, and flooding is a danger when south-easterly gales coincide with high-water spring tides.

The 186-mile (299-km) Pembrokeshire National Trail ends at the mouth of the little stream **G** that also marks the boundary of the National Park. Two stone bollards mark the spot, across the road from the 16th-century New Inn pub, at the eastern end of Amroth beach **H**.

The storm beach at Amroth.

Public transport

Tenby (on route) 🚌, 🚆
Saundersfoot (on route) 🚌; (off route, 2 miles/3.2 km inland) 🚆
Wiseman's Bridge (on route): 🚌
Amroth (on route) 🚌
Taxis: Tenby, Saundersfoot, Carmarthen

Refreshments and toilets

Tenby (on route) Good selection; Caffe Vista ☕, Bull Ball (restaurant)
Saundersfoot (on route) Coffee Tavern ☕; Mermaid on the Strand (restaurant)
Wiseman's Bridge Wiseman's Bridge Inn 🍺
Amroth (on route) New Inn 🍺, Amroth Arms 🍺, The Pirate Café ☕
Food shops: Tenby, Wiseman's Bridge, Saundersfoot
Public toilets: Tenby, Saundersfoot, Amroth

Accommodation

Amroth (on route) Mellieha Guest House, Amroth Bay Holidays Caravan Holiday Home
Tenby (on route) Cliffe Norton Hotel, Park Hotel
Narbeth (10 miles/16.1 km) The Grove, Bluestone Holiday Park
Saundersfoot (on route) St Brides Spa Hotel, Merlewood Hotel

2 Amroth to Laugharne (Talacharn)

via Marros Sands and Pendine
10.8 miles (17.4 km)

Ascent 722 feet (220 metres)
Highest point 410 feet (125 metres)

This stretch of coastline has some of the dramatic qualities of the Pembrokeshire coast to the west – including sweeping sandy beaches, rugged cliffs and high-level panoramic viewpoints – but attracts fewer tourists. It's a lovely welcome to tranquil, largely unspoilt Carmarthenshire and makes for a pleasant four or five hours of mainly high-level walking.

To get to the start of this walk using public transport, take a train to Tenby and take a taxi or the 351 bus (only one service on Sunday). The same bus continues to Pendine.

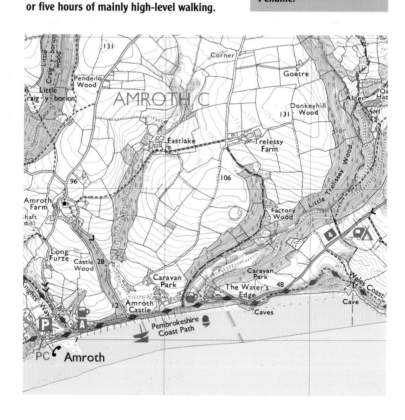

Look out for... prehistoric tree stumps on Marros Sands, Museum of Speed, Pendine Sands, Ginst Point.

Before setting off on the walk, you may want to take a look around Amroth, where there is an 18th-century mansion built on the site of a Norman castle (and so known as Amroth Castle), now used as the main house for a caravan and chalet site. There's a coffee shop on the grounds if you need a drink before setting off.

In the 19th century Amroth was a small-scale but busy iron ore and anthracite mining town and also shipped out coal from the mine at nearby Stepaside. A few remains of mines and tramways are still visible. Now the town is a village and something of a poor cousin to nearby Tenby and Saundersfoot, with a stony beach protected from erosion by a series of groynes. When the tide is at its lowest you should be able to see a petrified forest, destroyed when sea levels rose around 7,000 years ago; fossilised antlers, nuts, animal bones and Neolithic flints have also been discovered on Amroth beach.

This section is quite easy walking. Like much of the Pembrokeshire Coast Path, it is undulating but involves no major detours away from the coast to get round streams or inlets. After passing two long beaches – deserted Marros Sands and busier, bigger Pendine Sands – the path does, however, veer inland and use the roadside to get past the significant obstacle of an MoD firing range.

From the stone bollards **A** marking the end/beginning of the Pembrokeshire Coast Path, follow the gently upward-sloping main road eastwards – note the Wales Coast Path (WCP) waymark with its distinctive blue-and-yellow dragon-shell stuck somewhat discreetly on the traffic signpost – before turning right through a large gate into a field. Follow the clearly marked track through bracken and gorse. You will soon be high enough to see over to the Gower Peninsula, with Worm's Head standing out beyond the western tip of Rhossili.

The path now follows the top of the cliff, climbing gradually. At first only a hedgerow separates the path from the road but it eventually veers to the right, passing through patches of purple foxglove in spring and summer. The climb is gentle but the path then winds down a steep section, including a 75-step staircase.

Pass a four-way signpost, ignoring the wide path on your left; instead take the short, steep (40-step) staircase down to a wooden bridge across a stream. You will see the WCP waymark on an old stile and older signage that marks the border with Carmarthenshire.

Where Pembrokeshire is known as 'little England' and is firmly established as a holiday destination for English as well as Welsh tourists, Carmarthenshire is widely regarded as Wales's undiscovered county. The vegetation and terrain turns noticeably wilder from here on and you are likely to meet fewer walkers and day-trippers.

The path becomes a shallow trench for a few yards before following the non-dangerous edge of the cliff, followed by some gentle climbing up to a wooden bridge over a boggy stream. It then rises further to around 240 feet (73 metres) above sea level, with sweeping views over the wide beach (if the tide is out) of Marros Sands. Not a bathers' beach, due to possible rips on the rocks, this is nonetheless a beautiful stretch of sand; if you prefer a low-level walk you can opt to take one of the right turns off the WCP and walk along the beach. At low tide, tree stumps may be visible, evidence of a prehistoric forest **1**.

The WCP descends slowly, passing over a stile and then zigzagging down towards the beach, passing through a small copse. After crossing a short bridge over a brook and going through a gate, there's a steep climb back, then a gentler climb up to 300 feet (90 metres) above sea level – the highest point so far. This is a nice spot for a picnic, with views up the coast and – on a clear day – across the Bristol Channel to Devon, but no bench.

Next comes a steep descent, passing a path that leads down to Underhill Farm – and the beach – before bending left and climbing up to a bench, which offers a place to rest but affords no panoramic views. Five minutes further along there is a bench at a slightly loftier position with open vistas of the Gower and west to Tenby.

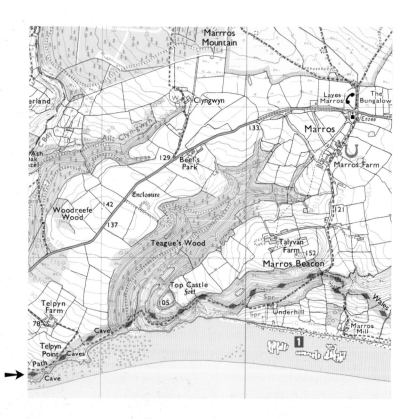

Empty and unspoiled: Marros Sands.

The path, passing under the telephone and power lines serving Underhill (and a second farm, Marros Hill, just to the west), goes through a gate, across an unmade road and then through a kissing-gate before becoming a switchback road to go through a second kissing-gate into a small patch of woodland. After crossing another stile, go over a brook and pass through another gate. You're now much closer to sea level and will be able to hear the sound of the waves. Shags are permanent residents on Marros Sands, and are often seen drying their wings at the edge of the surf. You may see anglers collecting lugworms for fishing bait or, if not, the patterns their gardening forks leave on the beach. Paragliders also use Marros Sands, taking advantage of the steady coastal thermals and the lack of people or major obstacles below.

On the right you'll see a narrow path down to the beach, but the coast path follows a boardwalk over a muddy patch of ground and then passes through a rather boggy boulder field. As you get higher up there are large rocks to sit on if you need a lunch or rest stop.

After this the path turns sharply, and quite steeply to the left, away from the beach, passing through a kissing-gate. The summit – 410 feet (125 metres) above sea level – is the highest point on the Amroth–Pendine section, with wonderful views across to Pendine Sands, famous as the

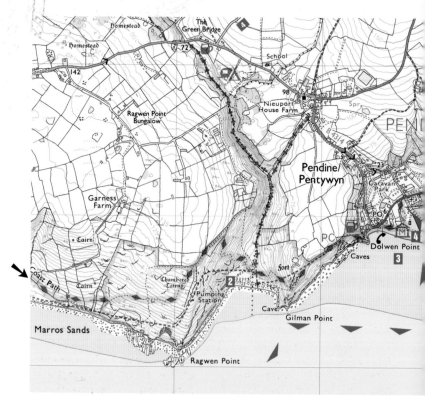

The Museum of Speed, home to Parry Thomas's big-engined 'Babs' car during the summer season.

site of several attempts on the land speed record during the 1920s, and across to the Tâf Estuary (see box, page 40). On a clear day, the Black Mountain, at the western end of the Brecon Beacons National Park, is also visible on the distant horizon.

The route becomes wide for a short section now, then turns right downhill along a narrow grassy footpath. There are stairs on the steeper sections, but in any case do take care as you go right down to sea level. The small pebble beach here is called Morfa Bychan and the jutting promontory on the right (or west) is Ragwen Point. The cove was bought by the National Trust to curb any further development; the sign says it is the 'last remaining undeveloped' stretch of coastline in this area. The land used to be overrun with Japanese knotweed but, after extensive conservation work, is now home to many native wild flowers and wild garlic (pungent in spring). Allied Forces practised on the beach in preparation for the Normandy landings in 1944; the long, reinforced concrete ruin that the footpath skirts was a bulwark **2** built to mimic the German defences on the French coast.

Just above Morfa Bychan on Gilman Point there's an Iron Age hill fort and the remnants of a medieval field system. The WCP crosses an unpaved road to pass through a stile and then attacks a steep ascent up to a third headland, the rocky promontory of Dolwen Point, where there's space to rest and recover on flat-topped rocks with stunning views east across Pendine Sands **3**. A staircase – not in the best state of repair – leads down to Pendine (Pentywyn); you are likely to meet some oncoming traffic here as holidaymakers from the resort's caravan sites like to do the short walk up to Dolwen Point.

At the foot of the staircase is the Point café. From here, follow the path past the shops and along the top of the seawall until you come to a B&B called The Beach. This unprepossessing building was the base for the land speed record, as recorded on a plaque built into the wall. A little way along is the Barnacle Beach Café and, behind it, the small Museum of Speed, which houses John Parry Thomas's car Babs during the summer months **4**; see page 40.

The beach here is open to the public and at weekends can be quite busy with bathers, picnickers and kite-buggy drivers. It is also used for triathlons and ultra-running competitions (the latter involve a 32-mile (51-km) round trip to Laugharne and back).

The beach is MoD property and officially there's firing from 8 a.m. till 6 p.m. Monday–Friday and whenever a red flag is flying. Land Rovers patrol the beach too. Note the warning signs about unexploded ordnance; don't touch anything you find that looks even slightly scary. At the weekends, unless there is a special warning (call the control tower at Pendine, 01994 452240, to check; or visit www.pendinesands.org), you can walk the length of the beach – it's 7 miles (11.3 km), though it might look like a lot less.

At weekends one option is to go to Laugharne along the beach and then walk along the right-of-way road through MoD property. This route, of similar length to the WCP, brings you back to the path at the end of the track leading to Salt House Farm **B** (see map, page 36).

The official WCP is not much fun for the next 2 miles (3.2 km) as it follows the busy A4066. Even where it isn't actually on the pavement it runs through fields and along hedgerows abutting this road – the main tourist route between Pendine and Laugharne and St Clears,

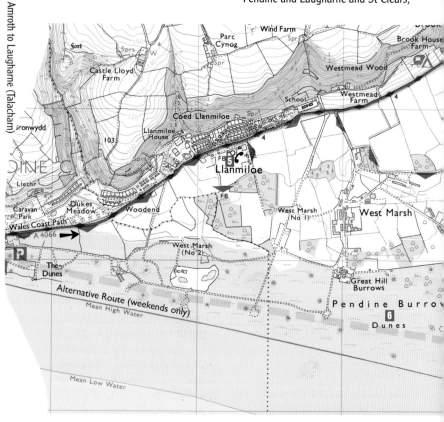

and used in summer by tourists driving to and from the M4.

Head away from the beach through the car park and, when you arrive at the main road, turn right. You'll see the dragon-shell waymark on a lamppost here. Follow the pavement past the Memorial Chapel and a shop/off-licence and then along the edge of the high chain-link fence demarcating the MoD Firing Range. Across the road is a huge static caravan and chalet site, with steep, wooded hills behind. The pavement widens to become a joint cycle/footpath, with some curious car-tyre-themed landscaping intended to beautify the roadside.

Around a mile on, in the neighbouring village of Llanmiloe, there's an interesting information panel **5** that summarises the links between this area of the coast and the British military. In 1940, when the MoD decided the testing range at Shoeburyness in Essex was too close to mainland Europe to escape the attention of Nazi spy planes, operations were transplanted to south-west Wales. The 18th-century mansion Llanmiloe House was requisitioned by the military in 1941 and became the officers' mess. After the war, the marshes were retained as a firing range and are now also used as a NATO European Region Test Centre (ERTC). As well as routine tests of small arms, there's a long test track used to study how missiles penetrate buildings and metalwork; you may see Chinooks delivering scientists or test equipment to the site.

While this has resulted in something of a no-man's land for walkers and tourists, it has helped protect the 6-mile (9.6-km) stretch of sand dunes known as Pendine Burrows, providing a habitat for otters, water voles, golden plovers and flora such as fen orchid and dune gentian. (If you are staying in Pendine or the area over a weekend you can visit the dunes from the beach side **6**.)

Shortly after the information panel, the path continues through some trees and crosses a short footbridge that fords a brook. The cycle path ends here but the WCP continues on through a small park with benches and lawns and through a car park past Llanmiloe's 'Post Office and Drug Store', a hairdresser's and an abandoned newsagent's.

Head towards the road after the car park and, at a very permanent-looking signpost for Bingo and Quiz nights at the local community centre, cross the road – with caution – and take the street on your right. About 100 yards (90 metres) along a path veers off to the right to take you back to the road. Follow the pavement for a few minutes, crossing the entrance to Woodlands Close (Y Goedlan) and then – again, carefully – re-cross the A4066 to enter a field.

From here the path runs for around half a mile through a series of (possibly boggy) fields, with the path either marked by a corridor of hedgerow and wire fencing, or by a slightly raised stone path or by nothing – in places the grass is very long and you have to sort of wade through it.

There are several footbridges, three stiles, and both farm gates and kissing-gates – and occasional waymarks – along the way, but if you keep close to the road at all times you won't go wrong. The only (very short) stretch on the actual road comes early on, when you have to use the grass shoulder to pass the long entrance to the main gate of the NATO/ERTC site, managed by defence and security firm QinetiQ.

The last field is higher and drier than the rest and, looking west, you will see several bungalows and a hill scarred on its top by quarrying. Ignore any gates that lead off to the road until you come to a high stile and wooden staircase that takes you up on to the roadside. The tiny hamlet here, Plashett, has a pretty Baptist chapel dating from 1862.

From here the 'path' is merely the grassy shoulder on the road, which curves and is fairly blind for drivers (who come at speed). When the verge is overgrown, as it often is, you may have to use the road, so be very careful for the next 1,100 yards (1 km). Ignore the footpath sign on the opposite side of the road: it will take you (up a very steep path) to Llansadurnen, which is far from the coast and some distance from Laugharne.

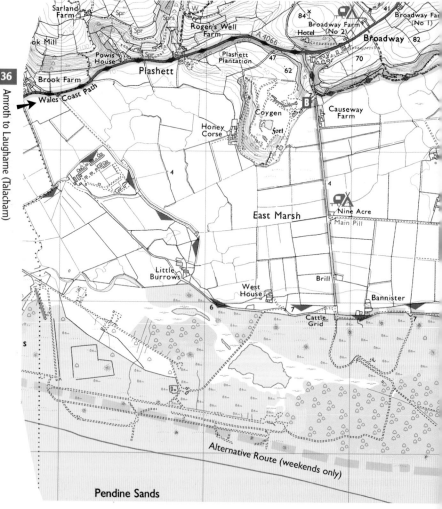

Following the A4066 around the sweeping bend, you will come to the sign marking the border of a village called Broadway and, pointing to the right, signs for Hurst House Hotel, a campsite and a B&B – and a WCP signpost. Follow this road down and, just past Causeway Cottage, turn left on to a farm track **B**, signposted for Salt House.

Salt House Farm on the marsh outside Laugharne, in all its autumn glory.

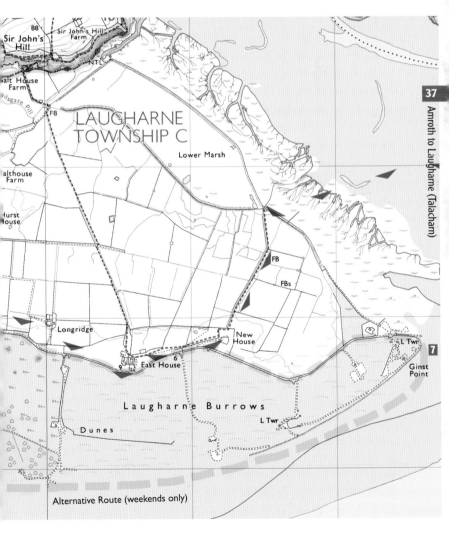

The stone marking the Dylan Thomas Birthday Walk at Laugharne.

From here on in, the coast path – while not exactly coastal, thanks to the MoD and the fact that there are extensive marshes all about here – is a pleasantly pastoral, traffic-free route all the way to Laugharne. Most of it is flat, with just one significant ascent.

After crossing the cattle grid, the track runs through grazing land and then arrives at another cattle grid. From here a fenced-in drive leads down to Salt House Farm (and its raucous dog kennels), the WCP veering right to pass the property and then becoming first grassier and then narrower. Bob Stevens, who owns Salt House Farm, is responsible for improving the footpath from his house all the way to Laugharne, with part of it now baptised as 'Dylan's Birthday Walk'. The poet is said to have hiked the path for his 30th birthday, a story told by signs erected by Bob and the Laugharne Corporation (the local council), featuring verses from Thomas's 'Poem in October', which he was inspired to write while out on this walk. You can read Bob's story at www.dylanthomasbirthdaywalk.co.uk.

After the farm, the path comes to a metal kissing-gate (the farm gate here may be open, though) and then runs directly below steep cliffs that drip with spring water, with ferns, ivy, brambles and wild flowers clinging to the cliff bottom. Some of the rocks are grassed over and provide an opportunity for a sit-down and rest. The path narrows as it skirts the marshes and there are increasingly good views of the Llansteffan Peninsula. Ignore any paths that lead right towards the marshes: tides and soft sand make this terrain especially treacherous.

When the rocky headland blocks any further progress along the cliff bottom, there's a stile and then a long, steep staircase (64 steps) and then a short, gentler section that takes you from 3 feet (1 metre) above sea-level to 88 feet (27 metres), where there is a stupendous view over the marsh and the Tâf (pronounced 'Tarv') Estuary – and a perfectly positioned bench. Note the tower far out at the edge of the marsh at Ginst Point **7** (see map, page 37): this is military land, but you can walk here at the weekend (either by walking from Pendine or by going through the entrance when the barrier is up).

There's a very short, steep walk up to a higher point, where there's another bench and open views across the estuary and, left, to the edge of Laugharne. A final, tiny climb takes you to the highest point in the Pendine–Laugharne section of the walk (150 feet or 46 metres above sea level), and you get another bench, and views, from left to right, of Dylan Thomas's home, the Boathouse (the small white cottage nearest to the shore), the Llansteffan Peninsula and, far to the right, the beach of Cefn Sidan.

The path leading off up the hill here is a route to the top of Sir John's Hill, a nice one-hour circular walk if you happen to be staying in Laugharne; see box, page 44.

From here it's all pretty much downhill, through shaded woodland, to the foreshore at Laugharne, with two benches, 20 steps, one gate and (probably) the perfume of the local sewage treatment plant to send you on your way. At the foot of the hill, turn left and follow the pavement round past the car park until you get to a stone bridge – note the WCP signpost – that crosses a fast-flowing stream.

Behind you is the Grist **8**, with two restaurant-cum-teashops, a pub, a small supermarket plus (pay-for) ATM machine, and a souvenir shop. Follow the main road up to the right to enter the castle or to see Brown's Hotel and visit the New Three Mariners pub.

Public transport
Pendine (on route) 🚌
Taxis: Tenby, Carmarthen

Refreshments and toilets
Pendine (on route) Springwell Inn 🍺
Laugharne (on route) Good selection; Dylan Thomas Boathouse tea room ☕
Food shops: Pendine, Laugharne
Public toilets: Pendine, Laugharne

Accommodation
Marros (0.6 miles/1km) Garden Lodge
Pendine Sands (on route) Pendine Sands Holiday Park, Springwell Inn
Laugharne (on route) Boat House B&B, Brown's Hotel

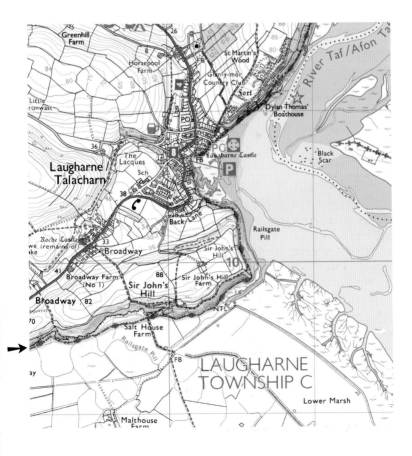

When the 'Fast Set' came to Pendine

Between 1898 and 1914 the world land speed record shot up from 39.24 miles per hour to 124.09 miles per hour. The latter was achieved by British driver L. G. 'Cupid' Hornsted in a 200-horsepower Benz car at the purpose-built Brooklands race circuit in Weybridge, Surrey. Prior to this, however, all but one of the records had been taken in France or in the USA and most of the drivers had also been American or French.

The shift to Britain signalled the start of a new era in racing in which British (or British-based) drivers would set record after record. As the Edwardian era came to a close, the sons of Empire were busy conquering Antarctica, flying across the Atlantic and scaling Mount Everest. As cars got faster and flashier, the upper-classes gave up their horses and carriages

and bought Daimlers and Wolseleys; they soon came to regard the land speed record as an endeavour worthy of heroes.

Hornsted's record established the mile as the new distance over which the speed had to be achieved and also established a regulation that it had to be measured over two runs (called 'passes') in opposite directions – to prove that wind speed was not a key factor.

But as the speeds increased, Brooklands – even with its half-mile-long Railway Straight – was no match for the increasingly powerful engines and a new, flat, firm, open track was needed.

The unusually wide beach at Pendine Sands, with its 7 miles (11.3 km) of level and – on dry days – firm white sand, looked ideal. In the early 1900s the beach had been used for car and motorcycle races and from 1922 the annual Welsh TT motorcycle event was

held there. Smoother and straighter than many major trunk roads of the time, Pendine attracted the best drivers and cars, which in turn drew large crowds of spectators. *Motor Cycle* magazine described the sands as 'the finest natural speedway imaginable'.

The first speedster to use Pendine for the land speed record was Malcolm Campbell, a public-school-educated son of a Hatton Garden diamond merchant. After working, unpaid, at Lloyd's of London for two years, Campbell gave up pretending he might enjoy a career in the City and took up motorcycle racing. After winning three London to Lands End rallies, he became a Brooklands regular and turned his attention to cars.

On 25 September 1924, at Pendine, Campbell set new records for the so-called flying mile (146.16 mph) as well as the flying kilometre (146.15 mph) in his 350-horsepower Sunbeam 'Blue

Malcolm Campbell and 'Blue Bird' at Pendine, 1927.

Bird'. On 21 July 1925, in the same car and again at Pendine, he broke his own record, clocking 150.76 mph over the mile and 150.86 mph over a kilometre.

Henry Segrave was an American-born, Eton-educated former fighter pilot who liked to brag that he would be the first driver to break the 200 mph barrier. On 16 March 1926, he set the land speed record over a kilometre in his 4-litre Sunbeam 'Tiger' on Southport beach at 152.3 mph. The car suffered supercharger failure during the record run and he did not break the mile record.

Carmarthenshire became the focus of attention once again when a Welsh driver decided to test his mettle on the beach there. Wrexham-born John Godfrey Parry Thomas was fascinated by engineering as a child, and went on to study it at London's City and Guilds College. In 1908, when he was just 24, he designed the infinite-ratio electrical transmission – considered years ahead of its time – and went on to join Leyland Motors as chief engineer. When he got to test a Leyland Eight luxury car – which he had designed – on the Brooklands circuit he discovered a passion for racing.

Unlike the rest of the Brooklands bunch, Parry Thomas was middle-class and quietly spoken verging on taciturn. But he was a meticulous scientist and engineer, carrying a slide rule with him

Pendine Sands' sweeping beach, as seen from Dolwen Point.

even when out at the theatre to make calculations during the lulls in action.

By 1925 he had given up his career with Leyland and bought a car called the Higham Special that had previously belonged to Count Louis Zborowski (who had died racing at Monza in 1924). The car was powered by a massive 450-horsepower, 27-litre Liberty V12 aero-engine, to which Parry Thomas added his own carburettors and pistons, renaming the car 'Babs'.

He took 'Babs' to Pendine Sands on 27 April 1926 for a world land speed record attempt. After a few warm-up runs he achieved a record speed of 169.29 mph. The next day he pushed the record over the 170 mph mark. Parry Thomas was on a roll, and 1926 turned out to be his year: he won lots of races and broke another eight speed records in October.

But, in 1927, learning that Segrave was about to attempt 200 mph at Daytona in Florida, Parry Thomas travelled once again to Pendine. On 3 March, despite being unwell with flu, he decided to take 'Babs' on to the beach. After his usual trial runs, he set out for a timed attempt. But the exposed chains that connected the engine to the wheels snapped off and flew into his neck and head. He was partially decapitated. Afterwards, commentators pointed to the weak chains in the car, to the limited resources available for engineers and drivers at Pendine's Beach Hotel, to the flu, and to the sands themselves – which are often not quite as firm or even as they appear.

In his marvellous 2004 book, *The Fast Set*, author Charles Jennings calls Parry Thomas 'something of a John the Baptist figure', not only for the manner of his death but in the way he was a forerunner of greater legends. Segrave and Campbell, and also John Cobb and George Eyston, went on to push the land speed record higher and higher, with Cobb hitting a remarkable 394.19 mph in 1947 – though soon afterwards rocket-powered vehicles would make the early records look almost quaint.

With Parry Thomas's passing, Pendine's moment in the spotlight also came to an end, as the action moved to Daytona and to the Bonneville Salt Flats in Utah.

'Babs' was buried at Pendine Sands at the site of Parry Thomas's death, but the car was recovered years later and restored. During the summer it is on display at Pendine's Museum of Speed.

Parry Thomas and 'Babs' break the record at Pendine in 1926.

Dylan Thomas's writing shed above the estuary at Laugharne.

Laugharne
The 'legendary lazy little black magical bedlam by the sea'

The little township of Laugharne (pronounced 'Larn') has a richer history than you might think at first sight. At the confluence of the Corran and Tâf rivers, it is referred to as both Abercorran (*aber* means river mouth or confluence) and Talacharn (of obscure origin) by the medieval chronicler Gerald of Wales.

Flemish settlers moved to the area in the 12th century as part of Henry II's campaign to oust the Welsh from the coast. In 1291, the town received its charter from marcher lord Guy de Brian IV, who built the impressive castle. In the 16th century Sir John Perrot converted it into a Tudor mansion and the present ruin is a confusing mix of house and bulwark. It is thought that Laugharne had a significant port – receiving imports of tobacco from the New World among other things – and a large population until 1607, when it was destroyed by the Bristol Channel tsunami. This may also have led to the silting up of the harbour.

Since Guy de Brian's day the town has been governed by a corporation, at the head of which sits a portreeve, who is elected every two years and whose symbol of office is a chain of gold cockleshells. His committee is made up of aldermen known as burgesses, who are traditionally granted narrow strips of farmland – you may see evidence of these on your walks. Only Laugharne and Malmesbury in Wiltshire have retained the Royal Charter that allows them to be governed in this quasi-independent way.

The township – it's not a village because of the charter – is now best known as the home of Dylan Thomas during the last years of his life and as the inspiration for his 'play for voices' *Under Milk Wood* (where it is rebaptised as Llareggub – Bugger All, spelled backwards). Thomas called Laugharne a 'legendary lazy little black magical bedlam by the sea' and waxed lyrical about the 'heron-priested shore' of its estuary. (For more on Dylan Thomas, see box, page 128.) Other writers associated with Laugharne include Mary Wollstonecraft, Edward Thomas, Richard Hughes (author of *A High Wind in Jamaica*) and Kingsley Amis.

Two walks around Laugharne

Sir John's Hill

A popular walk with day-trippers is up and around Sir John's Hill. This easy walk takes an hour and gives you the opportunity to read some of Dylan Thomas's poems – on panels built for the so-called Dylan's Birthday Walk – if you missed them on your way into town.

To start, retrace your steps from the bridge and go round the foreshore and back up to the benches above the estuary. At the highest bench there is a fork where, instead of heading back down along the WCP, you should bear right and upwards. The path leads through overgrown nettles and brambles to a steep path on the right. Walk up this and over the stile and go across the hilltop via a stone stile in the hedge between two fields. This is Sir John's Hill, named after Sir John Perrot, the bastard son of Henry VIII.

To get back into Laugharne head for the right-hand corner of the second field and turn left down a narrow lane. Follow this for about 10 minutes and you'll come out on to the A4066. You can do a right here and follow the road – there's a pavement from the bend downwards – into Laugharne. But the best route is to cross the road, go up the steps into the Orchard Park estate and then veer right for a great view over Laugharne Castle and the Boathouse. Continue down the street here and you will come to a very steep pedestrianised lane – Stoneway Road – that takes you back to the Grist and two pubs in the centre of Laugharne. Cross the main road to get back to the bridge.

St Michael's Church and Delacorse

A second circular walk – this one with a strong Dylan Thomas theme – is a little longer but has fewer inclines. Start at the bridge but walk across the car park and go up the A4066 (Market Street) past the castle, round the bend, and up past Brown's Hotel, the pub where the poet liked to drink – it's now a small and rather smart hotel. Opposite is a second-hand and antiquarian bookshop (the owner, George Tremlett, co-wrote a biographical work with Dylan's widow, Caitlin) and, next door to that, a large Georgian house called Pelican, where Thomas's mother and father lived for a time.

Continue up the A4066 (now called King Street) and turn right up the cobbled lane just before St Michael's Church – you may want to make a detour into the graveyard to see the white cross marking Dylan and Caitlin Thomas's graves (see page 132).

Follow the lane for 700 yards (640 metres) to a T-junction, where you turn left. A few yards on is another T-junction; turn right here and walk another 700 yards (640 metres) all the way up to Delacorse, which has lovely gardens and an impressive vegetable patch.

From here, you follow the clearly marked WCP across fields and through shady woods all the way back to the Boathouse, where Dylan and Caitlin lived with their three children between 1949 and 1953, and the writing shed where the poet worked. Once you have passed the latter, take one of the two sets of steps back to the foreshore or, if the tide is in, follow Dylan's Walk, Cliff Road and Market Lane back to the bridge.

The Tâf Estuary as seen from Dylan's Birthday Walk on Sir John's Hill.

Brixtarw

Delacorse

Afon Taf/River Taff

Maesyderi

Glenview

Canon Parc

The Brambles

Mapsland

Delacorse Uchaf

Caravan Park

Hillside

Keepers Cottage

Ants Hill

Mean High Water

The Glen

MHW

PW

Dylans Lodges

Pembroke Lodges

Horsepool Farm

River Coran

Tenby Chalets

HOLLOWAY ROAD

GOSPORT STREET

KING STREET

PW

Ferrys Chalets

Country Club

PO

Milford Chalets

St Davids Chalets

NEWBRIDGE STREET

VICTORIA STREET

MARKET LANE

DUNCAN ST

FROGS ST

MARKET ST

THE LACQUES

THE BUTTS

THE GRIST

Sand

LAUGHARNE (TALACHARN)

Mean High Water

Black Scar

Rugby Football Ground

School

STONEWAY ROAD

Q PARK

A4066

The Strand

GOSPORT STREET

Back Lane

River Coran

Sand

Railsgate Pill

Gosport Farm

Quarry

Sir John's Hill

Sir John's Hill

Sir John's Hill Farm

Sir John's Hill Farm

Laugharne Sands

MHW

Sir John's Hill

via St Clears and Wharley Point
14.6 miles (23.5 km)

Ascent 505 feet (154 metres)
Highest point 22.5 feet (74 metres)

This next section is short and easy, but not hugely interesting. Start early and follow the path that leads from the bridge in front of Laugharne Castle. After the castle, if the tide is out you can choose to continue along the paved coast path – further along are two steep staircases; but if the tide is in, use the official WCP and follow the first incline you see, on your left.

From Monday to Saturday there are six daily bus services running between Carmarthen and Pendine, with stops at Laugharne; there are also three on Sundays: timetables at www.tafvalleycoaches.co.uk. A taxi from Carmarthen to Laugharne costs £25–£30.

Look out for... Laugharne Castle, Dylan Thomas's Boathouse and writing shed, Delacorse Gardens, Whitehill Down, the castle mound at Lower St Clears, pilgrims' tombs at St Michael's Church, Wharley Point, Scott's Bay, Llansteffan Castle

At the top of the incline is Market Lane. Pass the two cottages and a tiny studio, and follow the path to the right, past a cemetery and a house called Bay View, then turn right, following the sign indicating the Boathouse (ignore the higher road leading into the Seasons chalet complex). If you've already visited Dylan Thomas's Boathouse **1** and writing shed (see box, page 43), walk past these and continue along the road as it gets narrower, eventually becoming an unpaved footpath and entering woodland. Follow the path as it makes a long curve around the Tâf estuary and you will come to a big kissing-gate that leads into a meadow. On your right is the salt marsh and up

on the left are thick clumps of gorse; the path here, which keeps to the right, lower part of the meadow, can be quite boggy.

Five minutes along is a boardwalk and a metal gate, after which you cross another field to pass through a kissing-gate into the grounds of Delacorse, a lovely house that has a walled garden with a chamomile lawn, orchard, fernery and extensive organic kitchen garden. These are open to visitors by appointment as part of the National Gardens Scheme charity programme **2**.

The WCP passes through Delacorse and continues along an unpaved lane that climbs gently. After passing a US-style mailbox, take a right turn along a paved road towards a farm called Brixtarw. Go through the farmyard and cross over a stile on to a track, then walk for 5 minutes before going over another stile.

Now the track curves to the right and slopes down to a gate where, following the dragon-shell sign, you do a sharp left. The path here goes through a pretty glade, over a babbling brook on a footbridge, and takes you quite close to the river. A boardwalk has helpfully been built over a section where the ground is very soggy.

Go up six stairs and over a stile and walk along the bottom of the field, following the line of the hedge. Go over another stile and do the same, following the hedge. After this field there's a lever-type gate. Go through it and follow the hedge, then go over a stile, on to a boardwalk and into another shady wood.

After the wood you enter a field and go straight on. In the hedgerow here, Ⓐ ⚠, there's a sign (probably overgrown) that might give you the impression you have to machete your way through the hedges. You don't. Simply take a right and, keeping the hedge on your left, walk for 10–15 minutes along a wide,

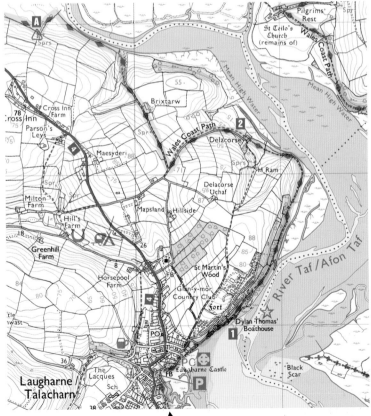

curving strip of set-aside (you'll see a dragon-shell sign on a post, eventually) until you arrive at the hedgerow along the A4066. Though it might look unprepossessing, the land you are skirting here is Whitehill Down **3**, a Site of Special Scientific Interest because it has rare species-rich grassland, with as many as 30 species of plant per square metre, including green-winged orchids, bird's-foot trefoil and great burnet. Between the 1930s and 1980s, 97 per cent of this habitat was lost, mainly to intensive agricultural improvement.

When you come to the top of the field, do not go on to the main road. Ignoring the two gates, follow the path – which may not be visible and may be boggy – along the edge of the hedgerow. Aim for the pylon ahead. Once you go under the high-tension lines, the land becomes untidy scrub and you cross a slippery bridge over a brook and then go over a stile. Here the path veers right to go round some houses. The signage is poor and the land boggy, so the best thing is to walk at around two o'clock after the stile and cross the brow of a field. Keep the pylon here to your left, go under the high-tension cables and phone lines and you'll find a newly built kissing-gate in the corner of the field. Follow the hedgerow in the next field and then bear left at eleven o clock (the river is quite close on your right now) towards another kissing-gate. Go through this, over a little bridge and through a gate into another field. Cross this and pass through another kissing-gate, then do a sharp left up a specially built fenced-in path to the roadside.

From here a series of purpose-built, clearly marked footpaths takes you into St Clears (Sanclêr), with some short sections on the road and two crossings

of the busy road and a stretch of pavement at the end. You actually arrive in Lower St Clears; the main, Upper, town is a 10-minute walk away, the two towns being divided by the busy A40.

There's not much actually to see in St Clears these days, but the town has a rich history. You'll probably feel that you're about as far from a coast as you could be here, but St Clears was not always so removed from the sea. A castle was built by the Normans in the 12th century, close to where the River Tâf meets the River Cynon (Welsh: Afon Cynin) – you can visit the impressive 26-foot (8-metre)-high oval mound of the medieval motte-and-bailey castle off Bridge Street (it's just a couple of minutes' walk up on the right and is visible from the road) **4**.

The town's name honours its 6th-century founder, Lady Santa Clara, and in medieval times it was a Marcher Borough – an independent district overseen by a Norman lord. In 1405 the castle was taken by Owain Glyndŵr, but he lost it the following year. During medieval times St Clears was a port, trading with Bristol, Ireland and France, and right up until the early 19th century the River Tâf could take ships of up to 500 tons. The town is on the main road – the A40 – to Pembroke Dock (and Ireland) and these days is a hub for traffic bound for south and south-west Wales.

The stretch of the WCP between St Clears and Llansteffan is probably the least interesting in this guide. Much of it is deep inland and through fields. The ground here is boggy and waterlogged, often grazed by uncastrated beef bulls (not generally dangerous but very curious and frisky) and the stiles, bridges and boardwalks – and there are too few of these – are in a state of poor repair. On the upside, it's a good workout and after Llansteffan the walk gets better.

To continue, turn right at the bridge and follow a grassy path that skirts the river behind the Manor Daf Bed and Breakfast and joins up with a street called Manor Daf Gardens. Pass St Clears Boating Club and then turn right across a road bridge. Go over a cattle grid (with a kissing-gate at the side), then over a stile and follow this road. Just where the road bends sharply to the right (towards a sewage works) you'll see, on your left, a double stile. Go over this and take a line at two'o clock across the field, towards the Pant-dwfn farmhouse above – watch out for bulls here.

You'll come to a stile in the top right-hand corner of the field. Go over this and follow a track around the farm, then go over another stile (with the dragon-shell on it) beside a farm gate and follow a wider track up to a modern barn.

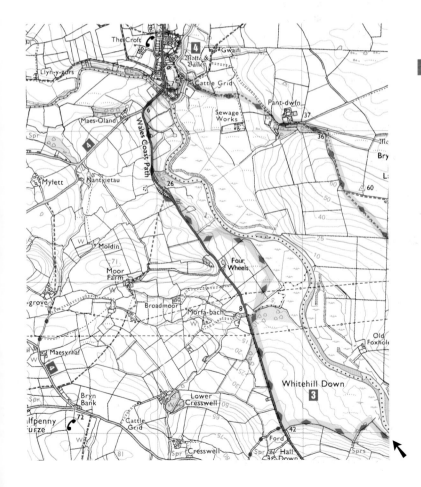

The dramatic ruins of Laugharne Castle, a patchwork of medieval fort and Tudor mansion. Authors Richard Hughes (*A High Wind in Jamaica*) and Dylan Thomas worked in the castle gazebo in the 1930s.

Turn right on to the road and then go through a farm gate on the right on to another track (do not use the farm gate into the fields). When you come to another gate into a field, go through and follow the track as it climbs beside a hedge on your right. Then go over a double stile in the hedge directly ahead into another field and take a route at eleven o'clock across the field to a stile in the corner.

The footpath passes to the right of a farm and follows a long, fairly straight line across three fields by way of several stiles. You'll soon see Foxhole Farmhouse on your left and, after passing under power lines, you'll cross another stile and step on to a little footbridge over a drainage ditch.

Turn right here and walk down the road, under a second set of power lines, into Trefenty Farm, a handsome double-pile house that overlooks the parishes of Laugharne, Llandilo-abercowin and Llanfihangel-abercowyn and the spot where the Cowyn (Cywyn) and Tâf rivers merge. Though much modified, the property was once the local manor house, owned by Sir John Perrot. To the west of the house are the remains of a motte-and-bailey castle.

The Wales Cost Path passes through the farm – note the old stone barns on your left and the dragon-shell waymark on a post beneath a tall tree – and then goes through a small gate, passes a stile on the right and then over a stile and over a double stile into a field. Go over the tump of the hill and you'll see the estuary in the distance.

Follow the (possibly poorly marked) path, aiming towards a big tree, which you will pass, keeping it on your right. Ignore the wide gate on the right and

head for the corner of the field, where there is a blue waymarker. Go over another double stile and continue straight down the next (possibly boggy) field, aiming for a stile that leads into a clump of trees.

The WCP in fact doesn't go over this stile – if you want to continue walking, do a sharp left – but you should make a brief stop here to see the ruins of the lichen-dappled St Michael's Church (Llanfihangel-abercywyn), a 19th-century building on a medieval site that is now overgrown with nettles and long grass **5**. You can wander around the ruins and what survives of the graveyard – three hogsback-style (i.e. raised) tombs, covered in moss, possibly housing the remains of pilgrims, are to the rear of the building. These feature distinctive symbols on the headstones and on one of the tombs is a cross, indicating a male grave.

Leave the churchyard through the same stile and then take a sharp right and walk into the corner of the field. Pass over two stiles and walk along the lower contours of the field. Aim always for the pylon straight ahead, keeping to the left of it, and then pass over a stile between a culverted brook and a steel gate.

Walk at one o'clock through the next field, which takes you under another overhead power line and on to two stiles and a footbridge over a brook; then continue at one o'clock. In the corner of the field, surrounded by trees, are two stiles separated by two 9-foot (3-metre)-long footbridges. After the second stile, do a sharp left and walk along the edge of the (possibly very waterlogged) field. Keep to the right of a short length of barbed-wire fence that has been erected here.

Go over a stile beside a WCP signpost and walk out on to a paved road. If it's been raining recently, you'll probably shout 'Hallelujah!' to be on asphalt – but don't, not yet, as there's more swamp to come.

Turn right and follow the road, crossing the River Cowyn (Cywyn), then turn right into the next field, heading through a kissing-gate to the right of a farm gate, back towards the estuary. Head at ten o'clock towards the river – the grass is

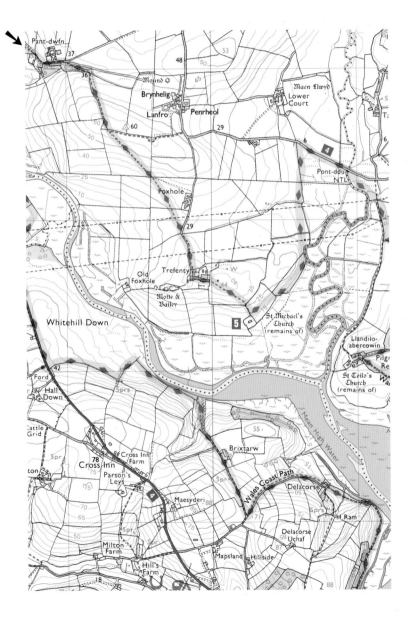

shorter here – and then follow the side of the river for a further 100 yards (90 metres) before bearing left towards a stile beside a metal gate beneath a pylon. It is exceptionally boggy here, so you may have to do a merry dance to avoid deep pools of river water and cow urine.

Turn right after the stile and aim for a metal gate in the middle of the far right side of the field. Enter the next field and keep to the left side, going straight on, and you'll find a kissing-gate hidden on your left. Use it or the wide gate – if left open – and go through to the next field and take a sharp right. Walk for 440 yards (400 metres) and then go through a kissing-gate to turn right on to a farm track.

Walk towards the farm (Llandilo-abercowin, on the site of another ruined church, St Teilo). In a patch of trees just before the main farm entrance, turn left (no WCP signage, but probably an old Carmarthenshire footpath badge) and you'll come to a farm track; turn left along this. Pass through a farm gate and you'll come to a wide, sloping field with good views across to the salt marshes off Laugharne. Walk straight ahead across the field and go over a battered old stile into woodland. Again, there's no WCP signage here. In the woods, you'll see signs of quarrying: the area around Llansteffan was once associated with quarrying the red marl, limestone and sandstone from the Devonian age from which the cliffs here are cut.

When you emerge from these shady woods, bear right and go down to a stile. Cross this and go on to the salt marsh. Keep to the left, walking straight on till you come to Cwm-celyn Farm. Go through the farm and keep walking along a paved road for 330 yards (300 metres).

Note the National Trust sign slightly buried away on your right. In 1997, the National Trust bought the 202 acres between Mwche and Pentowyn farms, recognising the importance of the salt marshes as a habitat for native and migratory wading birds. The tortoise beetle and a rare centipede have been found here too. Other features of the property include the remains of a single lime kiln and the ruins of a 19th-century belltower, used as a shelter and to summon the small ferry boat, which provided a link across the Tâf to Laugharne. Though the WCP mainly skirts the National Trust land, keep a lookout along the coastline for herons, shags, curlew, lapwing and shelduck, as well as ravens, peregrine falcons and kestrels.

After 220 yards (200 metres) turn right (there's a big WCP signpost here – the first for about half an hour) and go along the paved road. On your right are good views of Laugharne. Pass Mwche Farm, then turn right on to a track heading towards the estuary and Laugharne **B** ⚠. Turn off the road but go immediately through the farm gate to your left. Turn right and keep walking next to the barbed-wire fence till you come to a stile. Go over this and turn left into the field. From here on, you will follow the contour of the land for around 20 minutes. Walk across the field, cross over the stile and walk in the same direction across the centre of the next field. Go over a very high stile into a wooded area; don't go into the woodland but keep to the right of it, following the field round and then going over another stile, through a little copse and then up a grassy track between low trees. It's quite steep and probably overgrown. Turn right after crossing over the stile at the top and go through shady woodland along a level track, passing Pentowyn Farm on your right. Just towards the end, veer right down a track to a kissing gate. Go through this on to a paved road. (If you have time, take a right after Pentowyn Farm and in 20–30 minutes you will be down on the marsh **6** looking across to Dylan Thomas's Boathouse. Until the 1950s an open boat ferried passengers from here to Laugharne.)

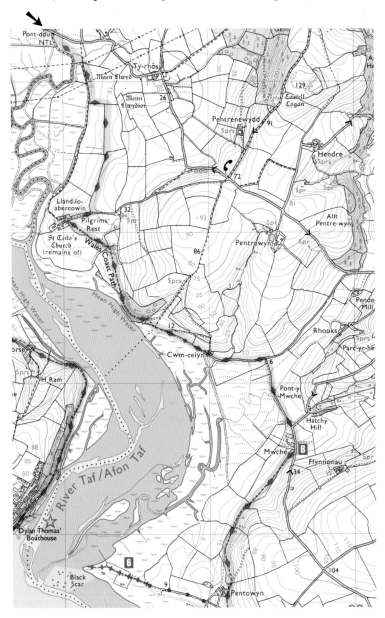

To remain on the WCP, turn left and follow the road for 1,200 yards (1.1 km) – it's quite a steep section, taking you up to 256 feet (78 metres) above sea level, and there are good views back to Caldey Island in the west and over to the Gower Peninsula to the south.

When you come to a crossroads, turn right; there's a WCP signpost here and another sign for Lacques Fawr Farm. Walking along this road you will be able to see – just – Llansteffan Castle popping over the top of the hedgerows on your left and, a little further along, stunning views of Ginst Point.

You'll soon come to a car park (and a bench) and the sign for Wharley Point. Walk on and then turn right on to a track. Further along is a stile and lever gate into the estate. Wharley Point encompasses beautiful woods on a headland at the confluence of the Tâf and Towy (Afon Tywi), and was acquired by the National Trust in 1983. For the next 1,400 yards (1.3 km) it's very easy walking on a single path along the coast, with good views, lots of benches and a couple of beaches.

Wharley Point, together with the adjoining properties of Lacques Fawr and Lord's Park, have been designated as a Site of Special Scientific Interest since 1987 due

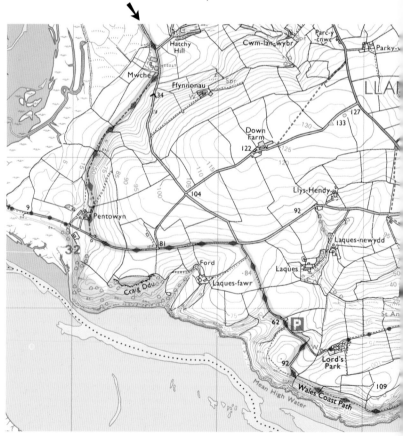

to their botanical and ornithological interest. A number of species of flora that require mild winter conditions are in evidence and there is a heronry as well as a peregrine falcon regularly nesting at one clifftop site. There are also the ruins of four lime kilns, probably dating from the 1840s; lime has been used for centuries in Wales as mortar and limewash for houses and also to reduce acidity and so increase fertility in soil.

Near sea level you'll come to a five-bar gate. There are paths to the left here to go back round the National Trust property and up to the castle , but the WCP forges ahead, past Scott's Bay – a lovely, secluded sandy beach – on the right and a pretty pale pink house on the left, and then climbs up a sloping path. Staying by the coast you'll come to a stone staircase; go down it, turn left and walk 330 yards (300 metres) and then turn right on to a paved footpath down to the beach. Here you'll come to the Beach Shop and Tea Room.

(Note: at the foot of the stone steps you can take a right down to the beach to walk along the sand into Lansteffan.)

Llansteffan is a good place to stop for refreshments, either on the front or in the village centre (along the High Street). Its castle **7**, which you should make time to visit, stands on a headland overlooking the sand flats at the mouth of the river Towy. The strategic importance of the location was recognised by the Normans, who established an earth-and-timber enclosure, or 'ringwork', inside the ancient defences of an Iron Age fort. The castle controlled an important river crossing and it changed hands several times. The transformation of the earth-and-timber stronghold into the masonry castle you see now was the work of the Camville family, who held the castle from the late 12th to the early 14th century. It was briefly in the control of Owain Glyndŵr's supporters in 1405–6.

Public transport
Lower St Clears (on route)
Llansteffan (on route)
Taxis: Carmarthen

Refreshments and toilets
Carmarthen (on route) Wide selection
St Clears (on route) St Clears Craft Centre café
Llansteffan (on route) Castle Inn, Pantyrathro Mansion, Yr Hen Dafarn, Beach Shop & Tea Room
Food shops: Llansteffan has a few village shops and post office
Public toilets: Llansteffan

Accommodation
St Clears (close to route) St Clears Travelodge
Llansteffan (on route) Bay Tree B&B, Castle Inn, Pantyrathro Mansion, Ger y Berllan

4 Llansteffan to Carmarthen (Caerfyrddin)

via Llangain

9.2 miles (14.8 km)

Ascent 2,205 feet (672 metres)

Highest point 333 feet (101 metres)

This section of the walk is intentionally shorter than the others because Carmarthen is the only significant town in the walk until Swansea, and is likely to be an entry (or exit) point for many walkers thanks to its good public transport links (regular trains to Manchester and to London and Cardiff, sometimes via Swansea). It also has plenty of historical interest – see box, page 64.

The 227 bus runs Carmarthen to Llansteffan and back seven times a day Monday to Saturday and three times a day on Sunday. Go to www.carmarthenshire.gov.uk and search for 'timetables' to find details.

Look out for ... Green Castle Woods, Carmarthen Castle

The village of Llansteffan was a port in the Middle Ages and, as well as local trade, would have been used by vessels from France and Spain carrying wine and other luxuries. Most bulk goods were moved by sea until the turnpike roads were built in the 18th century. Lansteffan was also an important centre for fishing and cockling – the latter persists in a small way and during the summer you may see cocklers' vessels out around the sandbar at low tide.

From the teashop walk on the path along the front and then turn left up Water Lane. Cross the B4132 at the crossroads beside Bethany Chapel. Go into Old School Road, but turn immediately right **A** up a steep lane that looks like someone's drive. Go

through a metal lever gate and head up a bridleway. After 170 yards (150 metres) go through two more gates – watch out here for cows crossing this narrow strip of land. You will find yourself walking in a kind of narrow, leafy corridor, along which you should keep climbing to pass through another gate and continue along a slightly wider channel-cum-path.

Keep on up this path and go through a lever type farm gate, soon passing Lan Farm on your left. Go through a gate and you'll come on to a farm track; continue straight ahead and turn right on to a paved road that goes downhill. After 470 yards (430 metres) you'll come to a road. Turn left and then turn right – before Dolau Farm – up a road marked dead end **B**. Turn right a little

A rainbow over the fields outside Llansteffan.

way up and go over two stiles to follow a track. Further along go over another stile and you'll come to two farm gates on your right – ignore these and go up into the field at eleven o'clock. Go over another stile and keep on walking – you're at around 262 feet (80 metres) above sea level here and there are good views down to the estuary and back to Llansteffan Castle.

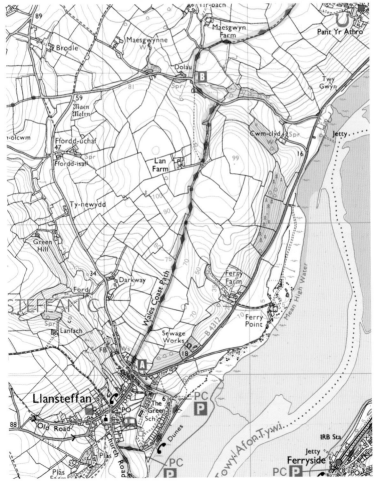

Some 380 yards (350 metres) along this field, keeping close to the hedgerow on your right, you'll come to a stile. Go over this and into another field. Walk on and in the acute angled corner of the field you'll find a stile. Cross this and turn sharp left up a stony track. About 110 yards (100 metres) along, turn right over a stile and into a field. Follow the hedgerow on your left. Go over a stile and continue down, then go over another stile and down through woodland. The path curves around and soon you'll come to a road. Turn right here and go down to the main road, then walk along the B4312 for 635 yards (580 metres) – there's only a short strip of pavement so take care

here **C** ⚠, especially as you go up the hill, as cars come fast. A dragon-shell sign now points right on to a steeply inclined lane (at two o'clock).

The lane soon levels out at around 262 feet (80 metres) above sea level, with some nice views over countryside but, alas, not much coast unless you find a gate on the right-hand side with views back up the Towy Estuary and to the castle at Llansteffan.

After 1,300 yards (1.2 km) you come to a three-way junction. Take the fork at two o'clock, with a sign pointing for the WCP and for Llety'r neuadd church. This lane goes under two sets of power lines, quite level now, arriving at the church

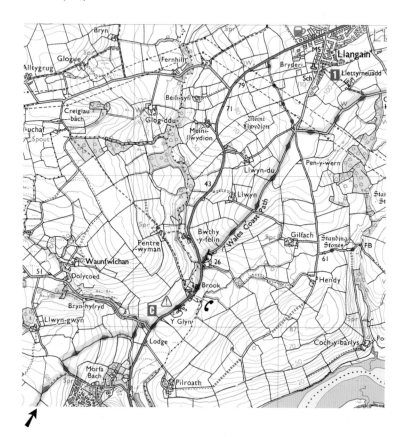

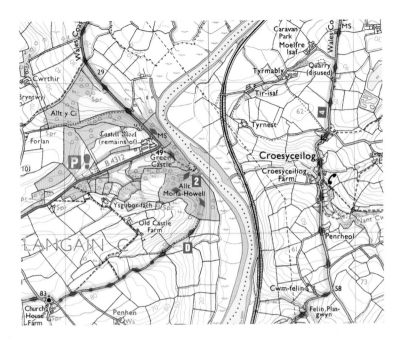

and a T-junction. You are bypassing the village of Llangain, associated with Dylan Thomas through his poem 'Fern Hill' which evokes his childhood holidays at a nearby farm of that name, owned at the time by his Aunt Annie and Uncle Jim **1**. Turn right and use the lane to the left of the churchyard, where there's a left turning up a wide track marked Church Farm (with a dead-end sign). Follow this and pass through a wide metal gate, then keep on down the hill for a further 660 yards (600 metres), passing a footpath and stile on the left.

Go through the gate here and over a stile, then down a track through two wide gates (the first one possibly open) and over two more stiles that ford a stream. After the second stile take a path at eleven o'clock (ignore the arrow suggesting one o'clock) **D** and walk through the field down towards woods

on your left. This land belongs to Church Farm, which has found time to put up a sign warning against bulls but no WCP signage.

Go over the stile into Green Castle Woods **2**, which consist of three separate ancient semi-natural wooded areas managed by the Woodland Trust in Wales (Coed Cadw). The trees are mainly oak, willow and alder, and there's varied ground flora such as wood anemone, wood sorrel, violets, wild garlic and bluebells. The main low-level path through the woods is the WCP (yellow dots mark the way), descending at one point almost to river level, where a short footbridge crosses a stream, before climbing up again (there's a bench to rest on here). You will cross the B4312 and then follow the path for some 10 minutes, through more woodland and through a hay meadow before coming back out on to the road.

Follow the B4312 (Llansteffan Road) for about a mile (1.6 km), past a golf driving range and a sewage works, until you arrive in the Carmarthen suburb of Johnstown. At Johnstown Football Club (opposite Rhydygors school) turn right into the playing field and walk for 140 yards (126 metres) along the hedge. Turn left to cross a track and a bridge, go through a kissing-gate and then bear left up a slope. Go through another kissing-gate and follow the tarmacked path to the right. This goes behind a leisure centre, then turns right to go through three more kissing-gates and on to a path (most of which is paved) all the way to Carmarthen. After 20 minutes you'll arrive at a boatyard. Go through it and you will come to a pedestrian bridge across the River Towy.

Public transport
Carmarthen (on route) ⇌,🚌

Refreshments and toilets
Carmarthen (on route) Good selection: The Spilman Restaurant, Poachers Rest, Restaurant 7teen & Deli
Food shops: Carmarthen
Public toilets: Carmarthen

Accommodation
Carmarthen (on route) Wide selection: contact the local tourist information centre; Falcon Hotel, Ivy Bush Hotel, Boars Head Hotel

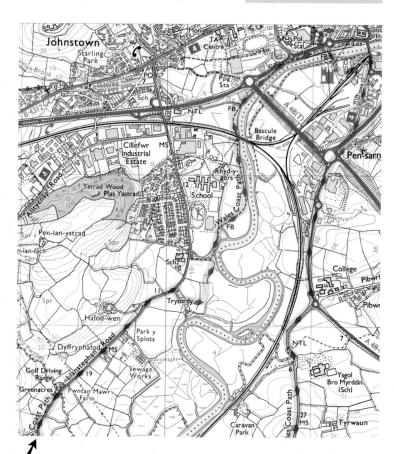

Ferociously proud of its Welshness: the county town's 10-foot-tall Red Dragon made from steel by Carmarthenshire sculptor Tony Woodman.

Carmarthen

Merlin's home and the oldest city in Wales – probably . . .

Some historians believe Carmarthen (Caerfyrddin) to be the 'oldest continually inhabited' town in Wales. During the Roman era, it was Moridunum, meaning 'sea fort' and the capital for the Demetae tribe. One of only seven surviving Roman amphitheatres in the United Kingdom sits on the A484, north-east of the town.

In the 11th century, William Fitz Baldwin, the Norman Sheriff of Devon, built a castle, which was destroyed by Llewellyn the Great in 1215. The present castle was built a little later and Carmarthen

became one of the first walled towns in Wales. The building has been modified many times over the centuries and was used as a county prison during the 18th and 19th centuries.

According to legend, Merlin (Myrddin) was born in a cave outside Carmarthen. Areas surrounding the town still allude to this, such as the nearby Bryn Myrddin (Merlin's Hill) and one off the shopping centres is called Merlin's Walk. A related legend left us a saying that, translated from Welsh, warns that when 'Merlin's Oak comes tumbling down, down shall

Castle, town hall and industrial units on the north bank of the River Towy in Carmarthen.

fall Carmarthen Town'. In order to avoid this apocalyptic end, the tree in question was dug up and preserved.

Located on the River Towy, the longest river to flow entirely inside Wales, Carmarthen grew around its inland port but has always remained an agricultural hub. Wool and woollen yarn, in particular, brought riches from the 16th century up to modern times. As the only major settlement in the region, the town has long been an important administrative and judicial centre for south-west Wales.

Though it has suffered from patchy development over the years, Carmarthen remains a pleasant urban centre ringed by fields. Look on a map and you'll see there are no other such towns in the area, meaning Carmarthen's pubs and restaurants are the focal point for drinkers and diners from across south Carmarthenshire. It's worth half a day to see the castle, Castle House (a former jail), the old velodrome in the park and the market. If you fancy an extra walk, the county museum – where you can see what's left of Merlin's Oak – is located in the old Bishop's Palace at Abergwili, 2.2 miles (3.5 km) east of the town centre; the sometime home of the Bishop of St David's, the house has been in use since the 13th century and it was here that the New Testament was first translated into Welsh.

5 Carmarthen (Caerfyrddin) to Kidwelly (Cydweli)

via Ferryside
14 miles (22.5 km)

Ascent 1,607 feet (490 metres)
Highest point 433 feet (132 metres)

With several hotels and plenty of pubs and restaurants, Carmarthen is a useful place to rest during the walk; if you don't intend staying over, try to leave 2–3 hours to see the main sites – see box, page 64.

Carmarthen (Caerfyrddin) is the main hub in the county for bus services and also has frequent trains to Llanelli and Swansea, regular trains to Cardiff and Manchester and one daily service direct to London Paddington. There are also trains to Fishguard, Milford Haven and Pembroke Dock, with connections for the ferry services to Ireland.

Look out for . . . Ferryside beach, Glan yr Afon Nature Reserve, Kidwelly Castle

To continue walking on the WCP, cross the King Morgan footbridge **A**, opened in 2005 and named after two local chemists, then turn left along the station forecourt. Don't go up the station's entrance ramp. Stay at track level and turn right at the foot of the ramp – waymarks for the WCP and Cycle Route 4 for Myrddin on a lamppost mark the point – and follow the path that takes you round the back of a railway siding.

This path sends you out on to a slip road. Keep walking for some 220 yards (200 metres), passing a used-car garage and going up to the main road, passing a bathroom and plumbing warehouse and – on the opposite side of the road – a branch of Kwik Fit. Pass the recycling centre and main post depot and, staying on the pavement, follow

the curve of a mini-roundabout that takes you under a flyover. After this, take a right turn up Emlyn Terrace, which takes you on to a cycle/footpath and through an underpass under another main road. A ramp at the other side of the underpass takes you on to a main road. Keep walking (there's a McDonald's across the road) until you come to a pedestrian crossing – cross here or at a cycle path a little further on, then keep walking in the same direction and you will find yourself on the pavement at the side of the A484.

Follow this till you come to a roundabout. The A484 heads off to the left but you need to cross the road and take the right-hand turning, as indicated by a tall dragon-shell signpost for the WCP and Cycle Route

4. Follow this pavement for 1.65 miles (2.65 km) and go over a bridge that tells you you're crossing the Afon Pibwr (usually called Nant Pibwr, *nant* meaning small river), shortly after which the pavement runs out. Use the road – with care – or the verge, of which there seems to be more on the right-hand side. In any case, the road is wide enough for two cars and there is unlikely to be much traffic here.

The King Morgan footbridge across the River Towy.

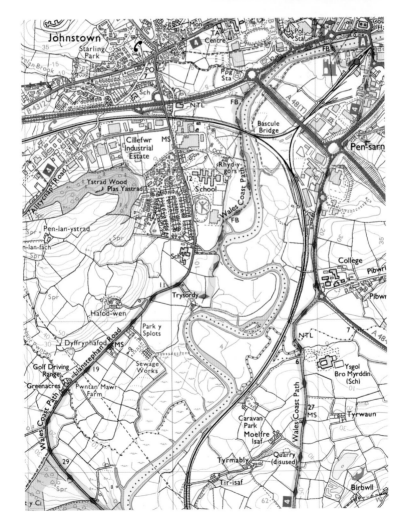

Terraced houses on the front at Ferryside, with the Llansteffan Peninsula in the background.

The road climbs gently to around 164 feet (50 metres) above sea level, entering the village of Croesyceiliog, where it bends to the right and winds down to some newer houses. Pass these and the bus stop (one service a week to Carmarthen!), then go up past a short terrace of old cottages. A further 10–15 minutes of walking takes you out of the village and up to a right turn, marked by a WCP signpost and a dead-end sign.

Turn here – you can spy the river down below now – and follow this for 1,260 yards (1.15 km), ignoring all farm gates and farm entrances. The lane becomes a farm track, hemmed in by tall hedgerows but with occasional views over the Towy **B**. At the higher points you can see across the valley to Llansteffan Castle – opposite your destination, Ferryside. Pylons stride across the valley floor but the view is still attractive.

This track comes to a metal farm gate; go through it to continue on a track beside a field, crossing a bridge over a rushing stream, after which you turn right, staying on the main track, up past a ruined farmhouse. A short walk across a patch of field – keep to the right – takes you to a stile; cross this and go over a footbridge across a muddy brook.

Go over another stile into an open field. Though the low WCP signpost suggests you might do a sharp right here through a gate, don't **C**. Instead, climb the hill, keeping on the right-hand side of the field for around 140 yards (130 metres) and you will come to a dragon-shell sign and an arrow pointing 90 degrees to the right. Go through the newish farm gate here and follow the fence that's on your left-hand side to pass through a wooden gate. Then follow this field up to the lemon-coloured buildings. Keep to the right of the field with fencing immediately to your right.

Go over a stile directly ahead to enter the farm area, then veer left, going round the conservatory-type building and crossing a car park to go through a wide gate (bearing the name The Old Farmhouse) and emerge on a paved lane. Head up this sloping lane, then do a left at the junction **D** (marked by Towy Castle House and a residential home). Follow the well-tended verge and then turn right at the T-junction. Follow the lane – note the waterwheel and bridge in the garden to your right – and you will come to the entrance for a handsome country house called Gellylednais. Enter this property through the main gate and head for a stone staircase a few yards ahead. Go up these steps and then turn left to climb

over a high stile under a pretty pergola covered in leaves. A lower stile is next, which takes you into a field. Keep to the right here and walk under the telephone lines. In the far corner, inside a dense clump of trees, is a stile somewhat obscured by tall nettles. Pass over this, cross the lane and follow a barely visible path through nettles and other wild plants just to the right-hand side of a dragon-shell sign. Climb over the stile here and go into the field.

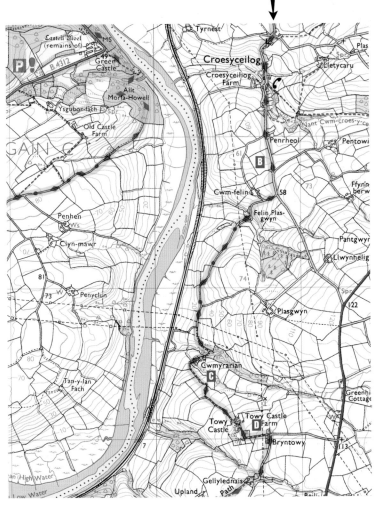

The beach at Ferryside.

and then following a hedgerow for a further 220 yards (200 metres) or so. After the next stile you pass the breezeblock wall of Pentrecwm Farm and go out on to a lane.

Follow this winding lane for 34 minutes or 1.75 miles (2.8 km), passing over a crossroads, but taking the right turn at the junction of Trelymsi Farm. The road now rises to around 262 feet (80 metres) above sea level, affording views of Llansteffan and glimpses of the river, before dropping towards the railway line and the salt marshes – the reason you are not walking the coast proper is

Cross this field, keeping to the left, close to a barbed-wire fence and under the trees (sadly, lots more nettles here). Hop over the stile and adjoining footbridge, then wade through the ferns for a minute or so on a path that runs at between one and two o'clock. Then use a steep staircase (53 steps) that takes you down to two bridges that cross a stream. This is a nice shady place for a rest or a snack.

After crossing the second bridge, turn right and go up the steps, over a stile and into a field. Cross this at one o'clock, as indicated by the arrow, and you'll come to two more stiles, close together. Cross these and go into another field – on your right you can see Carmarthen from here – and cross this. You will be in an open field at first

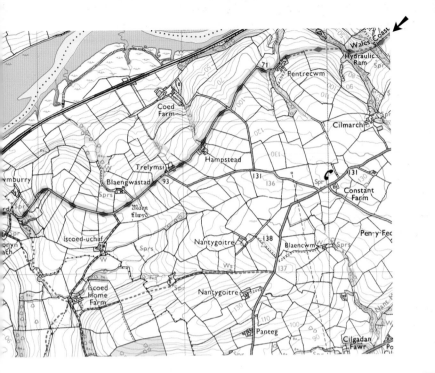

mainly because of Brunel's South Wales Railway, which opened in 1852 **1**.

After passing a honey farm, the lane leads into a beautiful wooded area and becomes more of a track. At river level (and below the level of the railway embankment) you'll come to a wide gate with the dragon-shell symbol on its left post. Go through this and walk straight ahead, winding between two white houses to find yourself on a paved track. From here you can see the Towy Boat Club on the opposite (Llansteffan) bank of the river. The path goes straight ahead (ignore the right turn that drops down to cross the track), accompanying the railway line and a few minutes along you will catch your first views of Ferryside and the estuary beyond.

Pass the sewage works and you will come to a main road. Turn right here, crossing a

stone bridge, and then use the pavement – or road – all the way to Ferryside railway station (request stops only). From the railway station, you are a short walk from the post office, pubs, restaurant and café and, immediately to the right, across the level crossing, is the beach.

Like the ferry between the Llansteffan Peninsula and Laugharne, the one that used to connect Ferryside with Llansteffan village no longer operates. Another former centre of cockling and fishing, it is now a quiet little place.

From the Ferry Cabin café-cum-restaurant, cross the road that turns on to the beach and go to the far end of the bus shelter opposite **E**. Look across the road and you'll see a narrow gap between two houses (a green footpath sign points the way). Cross the main road and go through this gap and up the path

The rare grasshopper warbler may be seen in the Glan yr Afon Nature Reserve on this section of the path.

that veers to the right, then turn right on to a shady cycle and footpath, which in turn becomes a road. Follow this, passing an over-the-top mock Tudorbethan block of apartments called Royston Court, ignoring the paths on your right that go back down to street level.

After 500 yards (450 metres) or so, the paved path/road ends and you are on a narrow footpath, between a wooden fence on the right and someone's garden. There are good views from here and a nice bench if you need a rest. Follow this narrow and rather lovely path as it climbs gradually and passes through a stand of ivy-clad sycamore and ash. Then descend to join a car-wide track that meets the road (called Port Way). Turn right here as if heading back to the coast at Ferryside but fork left up the single track 'coastal route' road (marked for Cycle Path 4), heading for Llansaint and Kidwelly.

Go up this road and, after the last house on the left, you'll come to a steep staircase **F**. Go up this to a stile and into a field. Ignore the track immediately to your right and go up

across the field at two o'clock, to pass through a kissing-gate. Cross this next field, keeping to the right, and you'll find a stile at the foot of a knobbly old tree. Go over this, walk a few metres and go through a metal gate.

Do a sharp right here, then walk along the bottom of a field to go through another gate into woodland. Cross a footbridge and curve left along the bank of a stream for 2 minutes until you come to a kissing-gate. Go through this and cross the road to go through another kissing-gate into a field which you should cross, as indicated by the yellow arrow, at eleven o'clock. Skirt the edges if the grass is too long to walk through and you will find an ungated gap in the hedgerow. This takes you into the next grassy field, which you should cross at eleven o'clock to go through another ungated gap, after which bear right, following the line of trees. Caution! There's no clear signage in this section **G**.

Head across this big field for 500 yards (450 metres), aiming for the opposite corner. You'll know you're doing the right thing as you need to be ascending here to just above 320 feet (100 metres) above sea level, so you will begin to see the sea and the Gower Peninsula. In the corner there is a car-wide track. Go down this and you'll find yourself beside a stone wall at the entrance of what looks like a tiny hamlet – it is in fact Pengay Farm: note the beautiful 18th-century barns, which you will walk past as you go down the road. On your right are views of the River Gwendraeth. Walk on and then go through a kissing-gate and down through a field at about eleven o'clock to cross a stile into a stand of sycamore. Steps here take you to about 197 feet (60 metres) above sea level (take care on the small lower steps) to cross a steam, after which you pass through a metal kissing-gate and out on to a sealed road.

Go left up the road and then up over a stile to climb a grassy path fringed by ferns into a clump of trees. Go over the stile here beside a holly tree, then up the right-hand side of the field, taking you back up to just over 320 feet (100 metres) above sea level. Cross a stile into a cluster of houses. Follow the one, roughly tarmacked, road past a huge barn, after which you turn left up a lane towards the village of Llansaint. Walk along a street called Heol Gwermont – note the turreted church up on your left – and after about 10 minutes you will come to a road. Turn right here and at

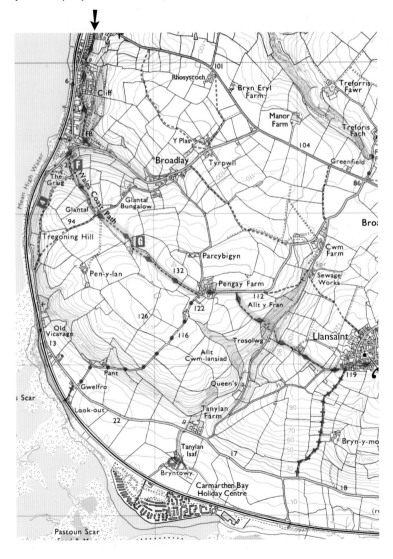

The silver, serpentining waters of the Gwendraeth Estuary.

the last house on your right, just before a public WC, turn right down a lane. There are good views of Pembrey Forest and west to Pendine and the Pembrokeshire coastline from here. A little later on you will get very good views of the swirling sands of the Gwendraeth.

Follow this lane (which soon becomes more of a track) for 600 yards (550 metres) until it ends at the driveway of a house called Parc-cwm. Here a grassy footpath leads direct ahead down the hillside between hedgerows. Where this ends, turn left down a muddy tractor track that winds all the way down to the main

road. A stream accompanies the last stretch, drowning out the noise of any traffic, but not the fighter jets and Apache helicopters that train along the coast here.

At the road make a left and walk on the roadside for 1,200 yards (1.1 km) – ignore the green public footpath sign pointing towards the railway line – and then turn right off the road, which here begins to climb gently, to follow a bike path (Cycle Route 4) into Kidwelly. This path is part of the Glan yr Afon Nature Reserve **2**, a habitat for reed and grasshopper warblers, curlew, teal and wigeon, as well as flora such as pyramidal orchids and St John's Wort.

There are a couple of nice benches here for a rest or to eat lunch. On your left you'll see the top of Kidwelly Castle **3**.

After 15 minutes, the bike path brings you out on Bridge Street at the Trinity Methodist Chapel. Turn right to cross the bridge over the Gwendraeth Fach (the bigger of the two branches of the Gwendraeth, though *fach* means 'small'), go past the imposing Capel Sul and at the junction with Station Road you have the Fishermans Arms pub, Kidwelly rugby club, WCs and the impressive St Mary's Church. This is the centre of Kidwelly – the station is a 15-minute walk down Station Road; services are infrequent and stop on demand (you wave to get the driver's attention).

Public transport
Ferryside (on route) ⇌ (on request) 🚌
Kidwelly (on route) ⇌ (on request) 🚌

Refreshments and toilets
Ferryside (on route) Three Rivers Hotel & Spa
Kidwelly (on route) White Lion Inn, Plough & Harrow, Time for Tea ☕, Anthony's Hotel
Food shops: Ferryside, Kidwelly
Public toilets: Llansaint, Kidwelly

Accommodation
Ferryside (on route) Three Rivers Hotel & Spa, Tanylan Farm Holidays touring and camping site
Kidwelly (on route) Kidwelly Bed & Breakfast, Jaron Bed & Breakfast, Old Forge Pumphouse Annexe

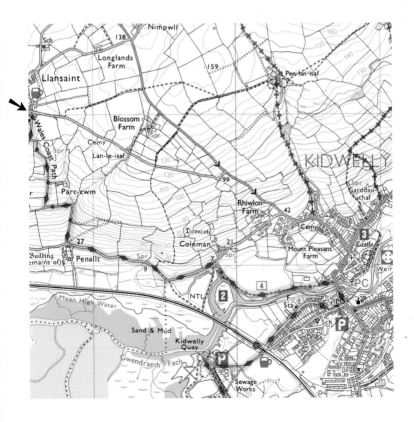

The magnificent ruins of Kidwelly Castle, built between the 13th and 15th centuries on a steep ridge overlooking the Gwendraeth.

6 Kidwelly (Cydweli) to Llanelli

via Pembrey and Burry Port

13.2 miles (21.4 km)

Ascent 564 feet (172 metres)

Highest point 85 feet (26 metres)

Make sure you visit Kidwelly Castle (which can be accessed from Castle Street) before setting off on the coast path. It is a very well-preserved, imposing structure. The earliest castle on the site was Norman and made of earth and timber, but by the 13th century it had been rebuilt in stone, following the half-moon form commonly adopted by the Normans. The great gatehouse was begun late in the 14th century but it wasn't completed until 1422, thanks in part to Owain Glyndŵr's efforts to stop it going up in the first place.

Kidwelly is served by buses from Llanelli, Swansea and Carmarthen and is on the West Wales rail line, though, like Ferryside, the fast trains don't stop here and slow trains only stop on request.

Kidwelly (Cydweli) could refer to 'the territory of a man called Cadwal', but may derive from the Welsh word for two river beds (*weli* is 'bed' and *cyd* is 'coming together') as the Gwendraeth Fach and Gwendraeth Fawr rivers meet here. Its coat of arms and official seal, however, show a black cat. The town has been spelt Cetgueli, Cadwely, Catwelli, Kadewely, Keddewelly, Kadwelye, Kedwelle over the centuries and it was not until the advent of printing that correct spelling became significant. The 'Cat' in 'Catwelli' may be the reason for the mysterious moggy, though some locals believe that Kidwelly was named after a local gentleman called Cattas, who was said to sleep inside an oak tree.

Look out for... Kidwelly Castle, Pembrey airfield, Cefn Sidan beach, Burry Port lighthouse, Millennium Coastal Path, Millennium Coastal Park, Sandy Water Park

This section of the walk leads from the Gwendraeth Estuary to the Loughor Estuary (a.k.a. Burry Estuary or Inlet) via Pembrey's sand-dune forests and the post-industrial landcapes of Llanelli. It's an easy, low-level section, the first part taking a long loop through Pembrey Forest and then following the 13.7-mile (22-km)-long Millennium Coastal Path via the 2,000-acre Millennium Coastal Park – the branding manager who came up with such similar names must have been sacked – at Llanelli.

From the T-junction at Bridge Street **A** walk down Station Road. Turn right at Hillfield Villas and walk for 10 minutes or so until you arrive at the Anthony Hotel and the railway station. Cross the railway line at the level crossing and continue along Quay Road till you reach a fork. Bear right and continue down to the car park at the quay **1** overlooking the upper Gwendraeth, a spot that is very popular with bird-watchers. From here a path heads south along the Kymer Canal.

Follow this until you come to a paved road. From here take the left-hand (east) bank of the canal and follow the gravel towpath for 800 yards (730 metres), ignoring signs and the bridges across the canal. Go through a gate at the end of the path and cross a field, keeping the hedge to your left. Note

the pillbox on the right. Walk on to go through a kissing-gate and turn left over a bridge to cross the railway line. Go through a wooden gate and a little way on you're on the A48/Pembrey Road. Follow the pavement along the road, passing a large car showroom. The pavement veers right at the round-about and goes over the Gwendraeth Fawr (meaning 'Large Gwendraeth', the – confusingly – smaller of the two branches of the river).

After 1.3 miles (2.1 km), a path on the right takes you under a low bridge (watch your head!) beneath the railway line. There's another pillbox on the right and anti-tank blocks, built in 1940–41, on the left here **2**. As you enter the

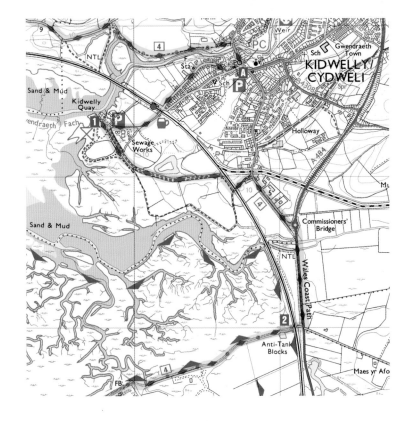

You might catch sight of the rare grizzled skipper in Pembrey Forest

wide open space, managed by the Wildfowl Trust, there are views back across to Pendine and Laugharne. The path has been raised above the salt marsh, which floods in spring tides, and runs around the airstrip: Pembrey West Wales airport **3**, which handles charter and helicopter flights, is the descendent of RAF Pembrey, built in 1937 and used as a Battle of Britain airfield during the Second World War. The airfield is within the MoD Danger Zone, because of the nearby Pembrey Sands Air Weapons Range. Built around the old runways is Pembrey Circuit **4**, a motorsport race track for cars (Formula 1 and 3 racing, and rally), motorcycles, trucks and go-karts which opened in 1989.

Other sporting attractions in the area include Ffos Las racecourse, a little further inland at Trimsaran, which opened in 2009 and holds National Hunt and flat fixtures.

Walk straight on for 1,400 yards (1.26 km) and at the end of the track turn down a staircase (16 steps) and follow a path as it turns right (this is signed as Cycle Route 4) and then heads straight on towards the forest. The path curves left and then does a sharp right and a sharp left and after about 1,300 yards (1.2 km) you go through a gate. Turn right up the single-lane paved road and walk into Pembrey Forest. The path soon forges left on to a narrower path that curves on to a straight path. Walk along this for 415 yards (380 metres) and then go left on to an earth and gravel path.

The next 2.5 miles (4 km) are on a clearly marked, wide path that goes through forest. It's not the most exciting of routes, and if you have time and energy you might want to wander off the main path along some of the grassy tracks to your left and right. Pembrey Forest, a sand-dune forest much prized by botanists and naturalists, is home to many rare botanical species. In May the forest – the managed part of which is mainly Corsican pine – is full of orchids, while in summer the show of evening primrose is impressive. The forest is the only site in Wales where the rare round-headed club rush grows in the wild. There are 35 species of butterfly here, including rarities such as the grizzled skipper, and the shrill carder bee is another rare resident. Many migrant songbirds, as well as birds of prey like the sparrowhawk and goshawk, have been observed here. Shy inhabitants include bats, badgers and brown hare.

A path off to the right will take you to a beach called Cefn Sidan **5**, which you may well have seen glowing during earlier stages of the walk around Pendine and Marros. The Welsh name means 'Silky Back', and it is a long, white sandy beach that glows when the western sun hits it.

The forest comes to an end at a caravan site. You will see signs for the beach and for Pembrey Country Park here; the latter charges an entrance fee and has play areas for children, a café, dry ski slopes and mountain-bike trails. A little way along is the car park – which you cross, passing the entrance to a skip company.

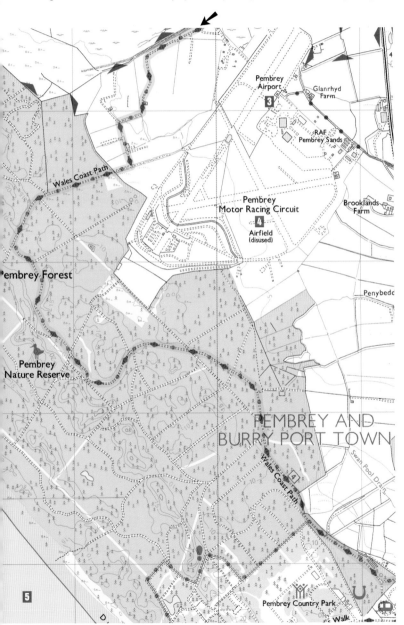

The village of Pembrey **6** – just off the coast path but visible from it – lies nearby. The 'mountain' (a hill) behind and Cefn Sidan are reputed to have been used by villagers who made their living as wreckers, drawing ships to their destruction by evil means – usually lighting fires to look like beacons. True or not, many ships were sunk off Pembrey and in 1828 *La Jeune Emma* was blown off course on her way from the West Indies to France and was lost off the shore here. One of the 13 (out of 19) passengers who perished was the 12-year-old niece of Napoleon Bonaparte's divorced wife Josephine de Beauharnais; she is buried at St Illtyd's Church in Pembrey.

Walk up the main drive (Factory Road) of the country park, with a links golf course (Ashburnham, used for the 2010 Welsh Open) on your left and a few minutes later you'll turn left between two stones

– Pembrey Gateway, the official entrance to the Millennium Coastal Path – and enter a very different landscape.

This is Pembrey Burrows and Saltings, a large dune system that, unusually for present-day Britain, is still being built up. On the left are the dunes, on the right a salt marsh that's wide open and wild-looking, with long grasses and no fencing. A nature reserve, it is a habitat for rare flora such as dune pansy, dune gentian and kidney vetch and the ungrazed salt marsh is home to the rock sea lavender, which fills the salt marsh with purple flowers in August. Golden samphire and sea aster flower in late summer. Birds to look out for include ringed plovers, skylarks, redwing, fieldfare and redshank.

Adding to the beauty of this stretch is the fact the Gower Peninsula is suddenly quite close. The path skirts a sandy inlet, becoming a raised path protected by boulders. About 1.3 miles (2.1 km) on

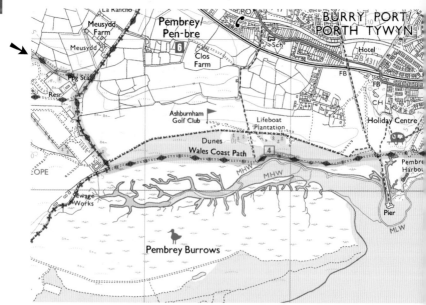

you leave the wilderness area and follow a path between dunes (to your right) and the Shoreline caravan site.

Follow this path, which curves left (at eleven o'clock) towards Burry Port (Porth Tywyn), cutting across a patch of wasteland, past a ruined house, and then up a tarmacked path to the harbour, once a thriving port full of ships loaded with coal from the nearby valleys. In 1928 it was the landing site for Amelia Earhart, the world's first female transatlantic aviator – in the town there is a rather lacklustre monument commemorating the event.

A right turn at the yacht club **B** leads to the Burry Port lighthouse **7**: Pembrey Sands were particularly treacherous for sailors and the lighthouse was built in 1842. On your left is the Lighthouse Café, which does hearty lunches and good coffee. The path turns left after the café and crosses two bridges over

wharves, then follows a tarmacked path, most of which is of a pinkish or rust colour, that goes all the way to Llanelli. This is the urban stretch of the Millennium Coastal Path, which is mainly built on post-industrial wasteland. The WCP follows this route and you can basically turn off your navigational skills and put away your maps for the next couple of hours.

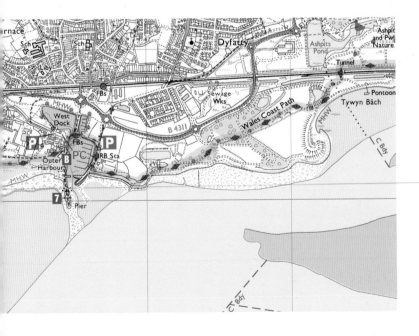

The Wales Coast Path passes through the Millennium Coastal Park at Llanelli.

There's another refreshment stop, the Pavilion Café at the Pwll cricket ground, about 2.2 miles (3.5 km) further on. A few minutes after this you go into the landscaped Millennium Coastal Park 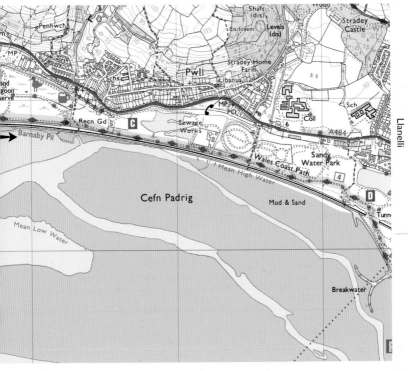 (not to be confused – though of course it often is – with the Millennium Coastal Path that runs through it). On the left is the Sandy Water Park, a 16-acre lake that is home to a resident flock of swans, followed by the Festival Fields, built for the 2000 National Eisteddfod.

At a brick monument atop a mound celebrating the building of the water park ◨, a path goes towards the centre of Carmarthenshire's biggest town, Llanelli (1 mile/1.6 km away), but the reddish tarmac of the coast path keeps to the right.

Public transport

Pembrey/Burry Port (on route) ⇌ (one station for both towns), 🚌
Llanelli (on route) ⇌/🚌

Refreshments and toilets

Burry Port (on route) Lighthouse Café ☕
Llanelli (on route) Good selection of pubs, restaurants and cafés; Sosban (restaurant)
Food shops: Burry Port, Llanelli
Public toilets: Burry Port, Llanelli

Accommodation

Pembrey (on route) Ashburnham Hotel
Llanelli (on route) Stradey Park Hotel, Coastal Path Guest House, Premier Inn Llanelli Central West, The Lodge

Llanelli

The town they called Tinopolis

Some walkers want their hikes to be green and natural, but one of the strengths – arguably – of the Wales Coast Path is that it runs through several industrial and post-industrial zones. The section from Burry Port to the Trostre steelworks, skirting Llanelli town centre, is an area of Carmarthenshire that has seen several stages of development, from cockles to coal and steel to the leisure 'industry' of today.

Ships sailed into Carmarthen Bay long before coal sailed out. From the Elizabethan era on, all the main harbours welcomed ships from England, Europe and the New World. Wool was exported; wines and tobacco were imported. The sea bed of the Bristol Channel is a cemetery of shipwrecks from the period. Cocklers have been harvesting the valuable bivalves for centuries and there has been a fishing industry since Roman times too.

There was limited coal mining in Llanelli in the latter part of the 17th century, but in 1747 Robert Morgan, an ironmaster from Carmarthen, leased lands from Sir Thomas Stepney at Llwyngyfarthwch and started working the local seams. Stepney himself became a pioneering industrialist, shipping coal into Europe and attracting English capital to the area.

In 1791, John Gevers and Thomas Ingman built a blast furnace a mile or so to the west of Llanelli – the suburb is now called Furnace – and four years later Londoner Alexander Raby took over the operation. Local lore has it that cannon balls for the Napoleonic wars

were fired here, and cannons have been found at Chatham Naval Dockyard bearing Raby's insignia. Remains of the furnace can be found in a picturesque valley called the Dingle.

The 19th century saw Llanelli explode – so to speak – as a centre of heavy industry. In 1802, Berwick-born Hugh Thompson Waddle set up a foundry and engineering works. In 1805 Daniel & Co. established copper works. To feed the foundries, coal pits opened at Erw Fawr and Box. In 1835, the Cambrian copper works opened and south-west Wales, especially the coastal stretch between Neath and Burry Port, soon became established as the copper-smelting powerhouse of Britain. The skyline changed: in 1839, the Llanelli Copper Company erected a stack 272 feet (83 metres) high. In 1860 a taller one, at 320 feet (97 metres), was built. Known as 'Y Stac Fawr' (the Big Stack), it was the tallest chimney in Britain for many years.

In 1839, the first stretch of railway opened, a venture overseen by the ambitious Llanelly Railway and Dock Company. Between 1850 and 1856, the South Wales Railway opened, connecting Llanelli and Swansea to London: the railway was built to ship coal from the south Wales valleys to London to complete Brunel's vision of linking London with New York.

By the end of the 19th century, Llanelli was producing half of the world's tinplate and had become famous around the world. The entrepreneurs who had built Tinopolis had made the coast one of the ugliest and dirtiest places in Wales, but the townsfolk accepted the environmental damage because it gave them jobs. At

Llanelli RFC (and now Scarlets regional rugby) matches the crowd sings the traditional folk song 'Sosban Fach' ('Little Saucepan') in celebration of the town's steelmaking heritage.

Llanelli is proud of its rugby team. Founded in the 1870s, the club is known as the Scarlets and has enjoyed many milestones over the years. None, however, can compare in the town's collective memory with 31 October 1972, when Llanelli beat the New Zealand All Blacks 9–3 at Stradey Park. In his poem '9–3', the comedian and entertainer Max Boyce wrote:

Now all the little babies in Llanelli from
now on,
Will be christened Roy or Carwyn,
Derek, Delme, Phil or John,
And in a hundred years from now they'll
sing a song for me,
About that day the scoreboard read
Llanelli 9–Seland Newydd 3.

As well as the great coach Carwyn James and Wales's first-choice lock Delme Thomas, alluded to above,

Llanelli has nurtured many rugby legends, including Jonathan Davies, Ieuean Evans and Barry John.

In 2003, when Welsh rugby became part of an international, regionally based league, the top-tier team became The Scarlets and Llanelli RFC became a 'feeder' team, playing in the locally based Welsh Premier Division; both clubs play at the newly built Parc Y Scarlets stadium.

Heavy industry staggered on into the early 1980s, but one by one the steel mills closed. Today the most obvious working examples of heavy industry are the Tata-owned Trostre tinplate plant and Dyfed Steel, a major engineering firm. In the 1990s, the vast industrial site along the front was cleaned up and transformed into the Sandy Water Park and Festival Fields, now part of the Millennium Coastal Park. Other attractions that have links to the past are the Sospan restaurant, which is in the old docks pump house, and Llanelly House, the recently opened heritage centre and genealogy showcase.

The All Blacks bear down on Llanelli's Phil Bennett – but the Welsh team triumphed over the visitors in their famous victory of 1972.

7 Llanelli to Pen-clawdd

via Loughor and Gowerton
11.4 miles (18.3 km)

Ascent 400 feet (122 metres)
Highest point 141 feet (43 metres)

There's not much call for maps or navigation for most of this stretch, as the path continues along the Millennium Coastal Path through Llanelli's Millennium Coastal Park. It then turns right on to the well-trodden but far more dramatic Gower Peninsula, the first area in the UK to be designated as an Area of Outstanding Natural Beauty in 1956.

Llanelli is served by trains from Cardiff, Swansea and West Wales, and by frequent buses from Swansea's Quadrant Bus Station and Carmarthen. It's probably one of the least touristy towns in the UK – the coastal path and park are its finest attractions – but has all the banks, cafés, pubs and restaurants you'd expect of a town this size, the largest in Carmarthenshire.

Look out for... Discovery Centre, Trostre steelworks, National Wetland Centre, arrival in the Gower Peninsula

From the path at the foot of the hill topped by the Sandy Water Park monument go over a hill, passing another monument **A** – a sort of pylon or obelisk symbolising the Millennium Coastal Park – and walk for 1,100 yards (990 metres) past some ugly blocks of flats. The Discovery Centre **1**, a tourist information centre with a café on the first floor, is next door.

A path continues on to the dunes here – and makes for a pleasant detour – but the Wales Coast Path turns left after the café, goes past the car park and then across two bridges around the North Dock. Follow the road for 10–15 minutes up to the Copperhouse

roundabout and then cross another bridge over an inlet. Here you turn back off the road and follow the coast path past some modern houses – ignoring paths on the left – and to a sign commemorating the 6th-century monastery of St Piro, who is thought to have founded a religious cell or monastery at Machynys, just south of present-day Llanelli. There is no concrete proof of the monastery's existence, but a large building at the same location was purchased by the Vaughan family of Pembrey in 1627 and remained in their possession until 1705. The family estate was then shared out between the heiresses, one of whom married leading local industrial kingpin Sir Thomas Stepney. Later on, the house was replaced by a farm building, which stood there until its demolition in the 1970s. All that remains now is a few remnants of wall and, legend has it, a secret tunnel linking Machynys with somewhere in Pen-clawdd on Gower.

An information display a little further along sums up Llanelli's industrial history and, rather neatly, as you walk on you will see the last few industrial sites still in operation – including the huge Tata-operated Trostre steelworks **2** (see map page 90) which manufacture tinplate used in tin cans, visible beyond the Machynys Peninsula golf course. A third sign records the disappearance of Bwlch y Gwynt, a village that stood here from 1880 to 1973 but was moved to make way for the golf course when the local industries dwindled.

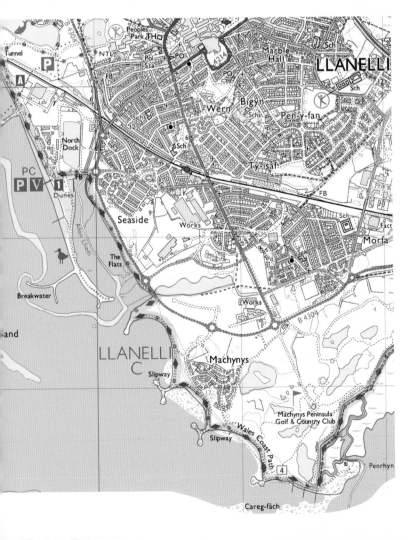

The path goes past a large pond and threads through a few narrow patches of woodland – there are quite a few benches along the Millennium Coastal Path if you want to stop for a picnic.

About 80 minutes – or 3.5 miles (5.6 km) – into the walk, with the steelworks now close, the path is fringed on the right-hand side by a flood barrier, built to protect the golf course. Staircases lead up to the wall of the barrier, affording panoramic views across the estuary of the Loughor (also known as the Burry Inlet) and to the Gower Peninsula. The path passes close to the Trostre plant and the busy B4304 here, so it could be quite noisy; but about another 950 yards (800 metres) along is the entrance to the

National Wetlands Centre **3**, a 450-acre nature reserve on the Burry Inlet. Managed by the Wildfowl and Wetlands Trust, the park contains lakes, scrapes, streams and lagoons – all themed around continents – with hides for observing clipped as well as wild birds (up to 50,000 strong), including swans, godwits, curlew, pintail, shoveler, snipe and little egrets. You may see wild species flying across the path as they move around the reserve. The centre has breeding populations of redshank, lapwing, reed warbler and reed bunting. There are also otter, water voles and several species of moth. You can use the café even if you don't want to see the birds (but the centre is a highlight of the walk and a visit is strongly recommended).

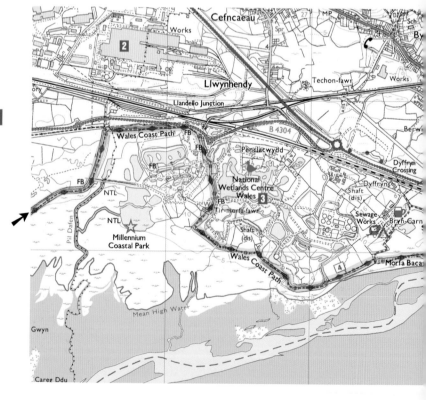

The WCP keeps to the left of the entrance and follows a tree-lined black tarmacked path. The next 1.9 miles (3 km) is easy, flat walking on a paved surface, taking you past the Gateway caravan site, along the foreshore (a couple of benches and picnic areas here) and across a footbridge 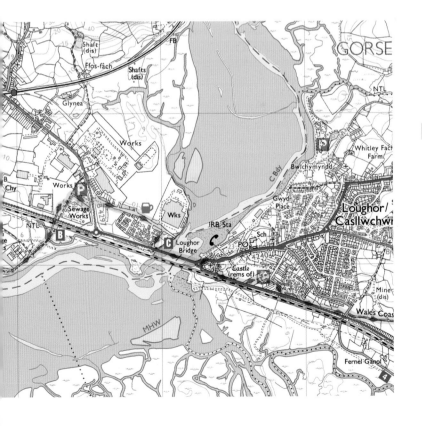 that gets you over the railway line and main road (A484). Turn left, walk for 2 minutes and then take a right, going round a sewage plant. Follow the path round the edge of a car park – Bynea Gate, the official end of the Millennium Coastal Path – and you'll come out on to the busy B4297.

You have to navigate again a little from here. Somehow you have to cross the Loughor, but don't be tempted to take a short cut using the roadside verges – it's dangerous. Follow the Wales Coast Path by crossing the B4297 to go up Yspitty Road. Keep to the pavement past a housing estate on your right, with the Lewis Arms pub on your left. After 550 yards (500 metres) you'll come to a large bearings factory (Schaeffer UK). Here a road on the right leads to a staircase up to the Loughor Bridge; where you come out is the exact line of the border between Carmarthenshire and the City and County of Swansea.

Cross the river and on the other side of the bridge turn left at the roundabout (the road for Loughor), crossing the road as indicated by the Cycle Route 4 sign (and the dragon-shell badge beneath). Turn left

Watching waders from inside one of the hides at the National Wetland Centre, near Llanelli.

and follow the pavement as it curves up to the right. You're on Castle Street, but for only a matter of minutes, and must turn up Station Road, past St Michael's Church, to arrive at a purpose-built cycle path that runs parallel to the A484. The first 440 yards (400 metres) take you through a park/playing field, then pass through a residential area and become a car-wide cycle path going past the backs of houses – all the time following the line of the main (and noisy) road.

The path comes to a road that you cross at eleven o'clock (ignore the Cycle Route 4 signs pointing under the bridge here) and follow the unpaved track up a slight incline. Ignore the farm gate on the right and keep on the narrow track. It's a noisy path – you can still hear the traffic on the road – but is pleasantly bosky. Ignore the stiles on each side of the path and keep on the main track; soon you will see the rooftops of Gowerton (Tre-gŵyr) up ahead. After 10 minutes you will come

out on to a back lane called Waun Road. Turn right here and walk down the road; ignore the metal public footpath sign pointing into a house called Eyri. In 5 minutes you will come down to a narrow bridge across the Lliw river **D**. Cross it and walk along this road, past a caravan site, with views across agricultural land on the lower hills of the east Gower to the right. Cross a little stone bridge and a minute later you come to traffic lights. A left turn here will take you down the B4295 into Gowerton, where there's a railway station, shops and a couple of B&Bs.

The next 1.5 miles (2.4 km), or 30–40 minutes of walking, is merely to get you most of the way to Pen-clawdd, but some of the views are rather good as the path climbs a little. (The path can be boggy; if it's been raining you may prefer to follow the B4295 to Pen-clawdd.) To follow the WCP, cross the B4295 and Bryn Y Mor Road and go up the footpath (no WCP sign) **E** alongside a culverted stream. A little way along, where a bridge turns left, the path turns right on to a wooded track (note the Gower Coast Path waymark here – it is also blue and yellow, by the way), which you should follow for 7–8 minutes. Ignore any paths off the main footpath and you will come to two little footbridges and a kissing-gate that takes you into a field. Cross the lower section of the field at twelve o'clock and go through another kissing-gate (beside a metal farm gate) on to a wider track. Almost immediately you'll come to a stile on a back road (its name is Cefn Stylle Road). Turn right on the road (there's a WCP here) and walk past a few houses, then turn left up Llwynmawr Lane. This soon comes to an end, seguing into a tree-shaded narrow path that climbs gently up to a metal gate and basic stile – though you can walk around the gate here, as there's no fencing.

Do not go down the lane here but stay high, keeping the white farmhouse on your right side. After you've crossed the farmyard, go through a metal farm gate into a field. Cross this at eleven o'clock – the views are suddenly a lot better now, as you see the marshes spread out below all along the estuary – and in the top corner is another gate. Go through it and cross this field at ten o'clock, going over a small hillock – it's 141 feet (43 metres) above sea level here and the highest place you will have

been for some time. You can see Llanelli, Burry Port and the previous 2–3 days' walk clearly.

In the corner of this field is a stile. Cross it, then cross another stile, heading downhill now. One more stile gets you on to a footpath through bracken, which in turn meets a farm track where you go straight on (by turning right on to the track). Follow this past a house called Bryn Y Mor and go down to a Chinese restaurant called Sea Garden **F**. You're back on the B4295. Cross it – carefully – and go a little way up on your right, where there's a locked gate but a permanent gap in a fence that you can go through to follow a cycle path

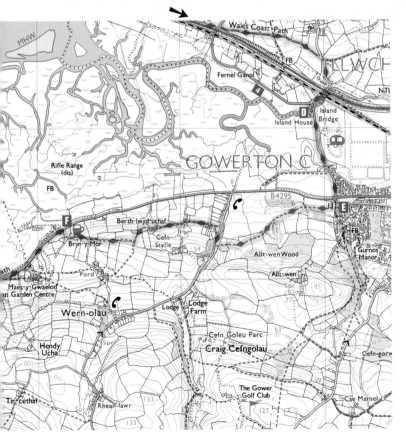

(parallel to the road). It's 1.5 miles (2.4 km) from here to Pen-clawdd's Presbyterian Tabernacle church 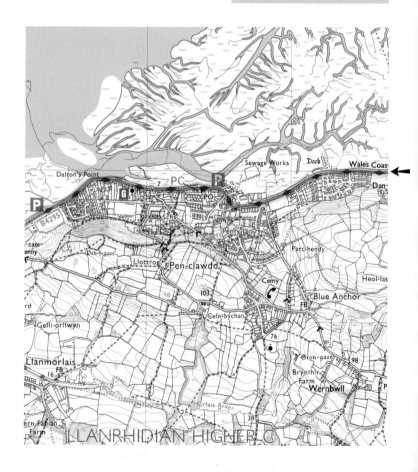.

The path (now on the pavement) winds through the small town of Pen-clawdd, and you'll pass pubs, a small supermarket, a café, a fish and chip shop and an Indian restaurant before coming to the front (Beach Road) and the church, next to the Bay View bed and breakfast. Pen-clawdd is famous in Wales for its cockles. If you stay at a B&B here or elsewhere in the Gower you may well be served cockles and laverbread, an edible littoral seaweed that is nothing like bread at all.

Public transport

Loughor (on route) 🚌
Gowerton (on route) 🚃/🚌
Pen-clawdd (on route) 🚌

Refreshments and toilets

Loughor (on route) Ship & Castle 🍺
Pen-clawdd (on route) Royal Oak 🍺
Food shops: Gowerton, Pen-clawdd
Public toilets: Pen-clawdd; also at National Wetlands Centre

Accommodation

Loughor (on route) Island House,
Pen-clawdd (on route) Bay View B&B, Old Manse

The main pill – or drainage canal – that cuts through the salt marshes at Pen-clawdd.

Llanelli to Pen-clawdd

via Crofty, Llanrhidian and Landimore
9.4 miles (15.1 km)

Ascent 393 feet (120 metres)
Highest point 225 feet (69 metres)

From now on the coast path is very well marked, and the text will feature less information about stiles and gates and try to do away with distances and logistical details so that you can concentrate on the lovely surroundings of the marshes and woodlands of north Gower. Look out for wetland and marsh species of bird such as snipe, redshank, rock pippits, plovers, sandpipers and oystercatchers from now on.

There are regular buses from Swansea's Quadrant Bus Station and Gowerton to Penclawdd.

Look out for... Llanrhidian Marsh, Weobley Castle,
Landimore Marsh and the marsh horses and saltmarsh lambs, Burry Pill,
Our Shop (Siop y Bobl) in Llanmadoc

Cockle harvesting at Pen-clawdd.

There's no green belt separating Pen-clawdd from Crofty, the next town along. Follow the pavement by the road along the front for 1,100 yards (1 km) and turn right down the first road (no road sign) you come to **A**, into Crofty Industrial Estate. After the Gower Vehicle Test Centre (a big green building on the right) you'll see a footpath **B** down to the marsh. Follow this path all the way round the outer edge of Crofty (which has a pub, the Crofty Inn, if you're in need of refreshment), past the sewage works, and in about 15 minutes you'll come to a playground after which you turn right. You now follow the road (Marsh Road) beside Llanrhidian Marsh **1** for 2.5 miles (4 km). The marsh belongs to the National Trust and is considered

Ponies out on the marshes near Llanrhidian.

to be one of the best examples of a salt marsh in Britain; it is of international importance due to the large population of wintering wildfowl and waders. You'll probably see horses, and the famous Gower saltmarsh lamb is also reared here. The area was an experimental firing range in the Second World War. A long concrete roadway extends out over the marsh, ending near an observation tower **2**, from which the accuracy and position of fired shells could be analysed. To this day unexploded shells are occasionally washed up on the beaches here, and because of this and the usual hazards of sodden, unstable marshland it's not advisable to go on to the marshes.

You will see several 'Walkers Beware' signs, advising that this 'Road [is] Liable to Flooding at High Tide'. It may be wise to check tides, but the only alternative if it is flooded is to use the B4295: not a lot of fun, as it's busy and noisy and there is not always a pavement to walk on.

In Llanrhidian (where there are pubs) turn right down Mill Lane (there's a WCP sign clearly visible beneath the church as you approach) and then bear left at Old Mill Cottage. Follow the WCP sign up a lane that soon becomes a dead end and puts you back on the marsh, all the way to Weobley Castle **3** (1.5 miles/ 2.4 km away) and Landimore (2.25 miles/3.6 km away).

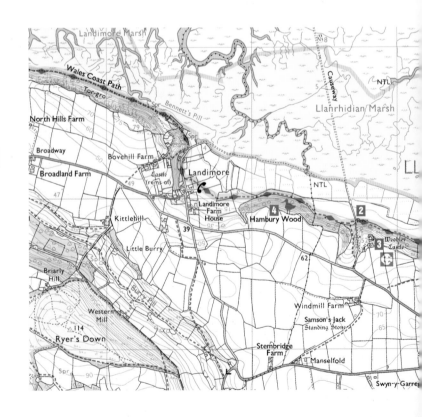

The early history of Weobley (pronounced 'web-lee') is obscure, though it was probably among the first Norman holdings in Gower. The earliest reference occurs in a charter of liberties issued in 1306. Later on it became the home of the wealthy and well-connected De la Bere family and is one of the few surviving fortified manor houses in Wales. Other owners over the centuries included Sir Rhys ap Thomas, ally of Henry VII, and the Mansel family, who also owned Oxwich Castle in south Gower.

After the castle, the path passes Hambury Wood **4**, an ancient woodland of oak and ash, with some maple, sycamore and dead or dying elm, managed by the Wildlife Trust of South and West Wales. A habitat to woodland birds such as marsh tit, nuthatch, and treecreeper, the wood was formerly known as Castle Wood, but was renamed in 1977 to honour Colonel Jo Hambury, the founding chairman of the trust. As the path approaches Landimore, it passes through some grazing land via several lever-type kissing-gates. The last of these will bring you out on to a paved road in Landimore, a tiny hamlet that once boasted its own castle.

Turn right and follow the road beneath the National Trust-managed Bove Hill (a rocky outcrop and the site of the castle ruins) on the left. About 500 yards (450 metres) along you come right down to the marsh again. Go through the lever-style kissing-gate and on to Landimore Marsh (also a National Trust property).

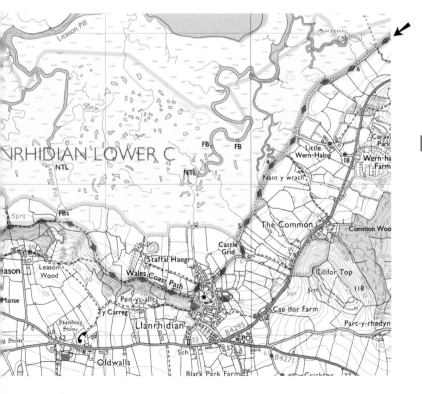

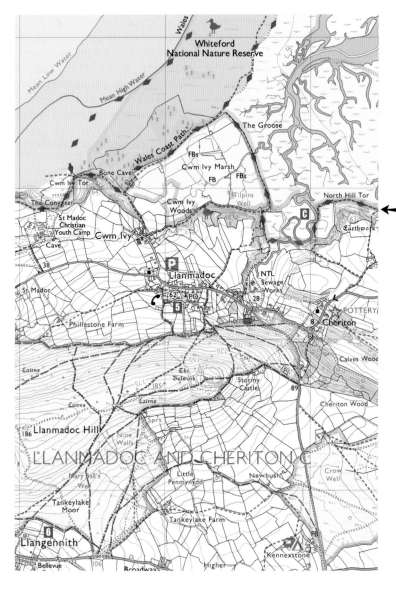

Though now mainly admired for their natural history, the marshes have played a vital economic and social role in the history of north Gower. Medieval settlements at Landimore and Bove Hill, Weobley, Llanrhidian and also at Leason and Wernffrwd – the latter two villages are just off the WCP – made use of the marshlands for grazing their livestock. A document of 1583 records that it was authorised for tenants of any Gower manor to put their animals to graze out on the salt marsh. The coastal location of the marshes also gave Gower inhabitants access to other resources, including food and transportation links to the Loughor Estuary. Landimore, Leason and Llanrhidian in particular are close to springs and pills – natural drainage ditches – that flow out into the estuary. At times these would have been navigable.

Walk along the marsh for almost a mile (1.5 km), until the track veers to the left. Here you'll see the village of Llanmadoc ahead and Llanmadoc Hill, the site of an Iron Age fort, behind it. Continue past the high-tide route and soon you will come to the newly installed stepping-stone blocks across the Burry Pill , a deep stream that runs all the way out to the estuary. Burry Pill, which once provided power for seven mills, still floods the marsh at very high tide, which is when you may be forced up the high-tide route.

Five minutes along is a lever gate. Go through this and, a little further on, you have the option of turning left and upwards to go into Llanmadoc, the only hamlet with a pub (the Britannia Inn) in this remote corner of the Gower (the road into Llanmadoc is a no-through road). There are also a couple of B&Bs and a wonderful community-run shop and café (Our Shop, or Siop y Bobl 5) and there is more accommodation 1.5 miles (2.4 km) away at Llangennith 6, which you can walk to over Llanmadoc Hill.

A right turn will take you out on to the low-tide route via Whiteford Point and its famous lighthouse.

Public transport
Crofty (on route)
Llanmadoc (on route)

Refreshments and toilets
Crofty (on route) Crofty Inn
Llanrhidian (on route) Welcome to Town Country Bistro
Llanmadoc (on route) Britannia Inn
Food shops: Llanmadoc's cooperative Our Shop

Accommodation
Llanrhidian (on route) Llanrhidian Holiday Park, Hillcrest, Oldwalls Farmhouse
Llanmadoc (very close to route) Tallizmand Guest House, Forge Cottage, Cwm Ivy Lodge (on route)

Recently built stepping stones facilitate crossing the Burry Pill beneath Llanmadoc.

The Glorious Gower

The Gower Peninsula is only 15 miles (24 km) long (east to west) and about 6 miles (9.6 km) wide (north to south), although the historic region of Gower once included a swathe of land much further inland to the north-east. The whole peninsula has been an Area of Outstanding Natural Beauty since 1956 – the Gower was the first AONB in the UK – and when you turn right at the edge of Gowerton or, indeed, approach via Mumbles and the sprawl that is Swansea, you know immediately you are entering an area of great rural beauty.

Until the outbreak of the Second World War, the peninsula was still largely a region of small farming communities with its own dialect and traditions. Its character was forged from its mix of Welsh, Somerset/north Devon and Norman ancestry and, like south Pembrokeshire, a significant English population.

Many words in the local dialect were similar to those found in the West Country. Even today, Gower can be divided into the so-called 'Welsherie' of the north, where Welsh was spoken, and the English- or 'Gower'-speaking districts – the south of Gower and Llangennith in the west.

A corn mill was established on Gower some time during the 12th century, as part of the estate belonging to the powerful Cambro-Norman Le Breos family, who were granted regional sovereignty by King John in 1203. The first written references to the mill appear in government records from around 1300 onwards.

The Le Breos' hold over Gower was under constant threat both from rebellion and from lawsuits, notably from the de Newburg family of Warwick, who had lost their land and estates to King John when he asserted his power as a guardian to a minor of the family.

The Norman rulers built Pennard Castle and shipped in farmers from north Devon and Somerset to replace the Welsh inhabitants. These initial ties with the opposite side of the Bristol Channel were to prove enduring, culminating in limestone trading between Gower and north Devon in the 18th and 19th centuries and the shipping of copper ore from Chile to Devon and Swansea in the 19th century.

The lie of the land

The peninsula's complex geology makes for a great variety of scenery in a relatively small area, from the south coast's carboniferous limestone scenery at Worm's Head and Oxwich Bay to the saltwater marshes and dune systems of the northern edges. Inland are large areas of common, dominated by sandstone heath ridges, including the dramatic sweep of Cefn Bryn. Secluded valleys protect deciduous forests, while the more open upland areas are still given over to agriculture – mainly arable and dairy livestock – and a patchwork of fields separated by walls, stone-faced banks and hedgerows. The AONB boasts three National Nature Reserves, two local nature reserves and several Sites of Special Scientific Interest and the National Trust owns four coastal properties on Gower.

Gower stirs all manner of passions. For middle-class Swansea residents, the peninsula is a much-loved back garden and an important recreational space – there are watersports and surfing beaches all along south Gower. For others, the Gower is, like parts of Pembrokeshire, a sort of 'little England', divorced from Welsh reality because of the reliance on tourism and incoming hoteliers and restaurateurs. But no one denies the beauty of the place, and the many well-trodden coastal paths now linked up by the WCP make the walking here easy, varied and, especially on the southern cliffs, very dramatic indeed.

Places to see and stay

As well as the sites mentioned in the main text, we strongly recommend you make small detours to see or stay at the following (for details, see pages 138–9):

The Gower Heritage Centre A rural-life museum and tourist information point on the site of a 12th-century water-powered saw mill – at Parkmill, just a 15-minute walk from Three Cliffs Bay.

Parc Le Breos In the 13th century, the Le Breos family established this deer park covering some 2,000 acres on land to the west of Parkmill. A Victorian hunting lodge, built on the same site, is now a beautiful B&B.

Fairyhill This small, secluded luxury hotel and fine-dining restaurant sits somewhat inland, near the village of Reynoldston, and is surrounded by gardens and woodland. It is well worth the detour and is a good example of why Londoners and other non-locals make the journey to Gower.

The Gower Way Created by the heritage charity the Gower Society in partnership with the Ramblers in 1998, this 35-mile (56-km) footpath runs from Penlle'r Castell near Ammanford to Rhossili. It's a great way to get high up and see the Gower interior, so different

from the coastal topography. En route you'll pass Bronze Age dolmens and Iron Age forts, medieval platform sites, holy wells, Norman castles and churches.

Pennard Castle Built in the 13th century, overlooking the valley that runs down to Three Cliffs Bay. Its location ultimately led to its downfall, as it was engulfed in sand and abandoned in the early 1400s. The ruins of St Mary's Church beside the castle can still be seen and remained in use until 1532. The castle is said to have been built – overnight – by a sorcerer trying to save himself from certain death at the hands of the Normans. Legend also holds that it is haunted by the ghost of an old winged witch who screams at anyone who spends the night there. A third myth, and the most popular, is that the castle's residents were in jubilant mood as they prepared for the marriage of Prince Rhys ap Iestyn. But when the prince, drunk, insulted the Tylwyth Teg people (Welsh fairies), they cast a spell and a huge sandstorm blew up – engulfing the castle and forcing the inhabitants to flee.

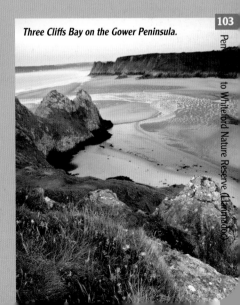

Three Cliffs Bay on the Gower Peninsula.

9 Whiteford National Nature Reserve (Llanmadoc) to Rhossili

via Whiteford Point and Cwm Ivy
9.8 miles (15.9 km)
High-tide walk via Bone Cave 7.2 miles (11.6 km)

Ascent 131 feet (40 metres)
Highest point 154 feet (47 metres)

From the village it is a short walk down to the entrance of the nature reserve. This could be a longish day, but the WCP now passes through the most dramatic section of the north Gower coast: dunes, some huge beaches, two small climbs and some high-altitude vistas – and a rusting lighthouse that is a wonderfully lyrical landmark. If you want to break the walk in two, you can turn inland at Hillend caravan park and go up the road to Llangennith, where there are B&Bs and a hotel.

> *There are up to six buses every day from Gowerton to Llanmadoc.*

Look out for . . . Whiteford Burrows, Whiteford Point lighthouse, Cwm Ivy Tor, Spaniard Rocks, Broughton Beach, Rhossili Common

From the lever gate **A** in Llanmadoc, turn right and pass a cottage to go through a kissing-gate into Whiteford National Nature Reserve (a.k.a. Whiteford Burrows). Walk about 880 yards (800 metres) until you come to a T-junction of paths **B**. A left here takes you to Cwm Ivy on the ordinary low-tide coast path via a bone cave (one of many such Gower caves where animal bones from the Pleistocene era have been found).

Do a right and you are adding a further 2.6 miles (4.2 km) by taking a route via the lighthouse – which is strongly recommended. The walk out to the lighthouse is clearly marked, skirting the marsh and passing through pine forests and dunes. The burrows or dunes are home to rare flora, such as early marsh orchid, fen orchid, early sand grass and dune gentian. Look out also for typical marsh birds, such as oystercatchers, knots, pintails and golden plovers, and for small copper, common blue and marbled white butterflies

After half an hour or so you come out on to a beach, where Europe's last remaining (non-operational) iron lighthouse stands **1**, close to the edge of the Loughor River. As the location of the lighthouse is 13 feet (4 metres) below sea level, you can visit it only when the tide is out, so make sure of your timing for the final 990-yard (900-metre) walk out to its base (a couple of hours on either side of low tide gives you plenty of time). It's well worth the visit, though, as it is a shell-encrusted, rusting, romantic ruin dating from 1865. You'll be surprised how close you are to Burry Port's more modern lighthouse when you get there.

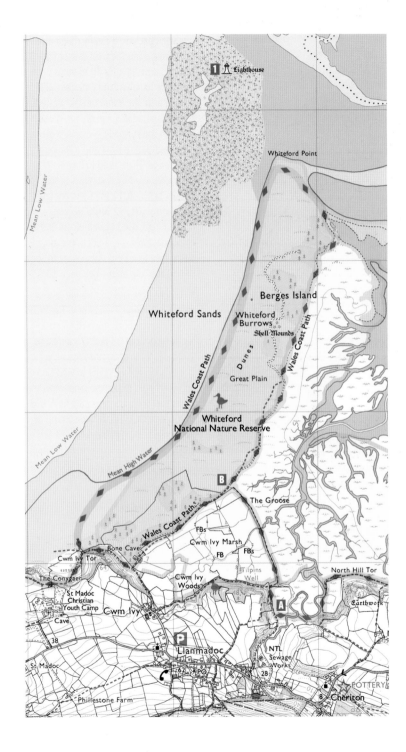

Low tide at Whiteford Point: the Victorian lighthouse.

The walk back on a clearly marked path takes you along the west side of the reserve, arriving after 20 minutes or so at Cwm Ivy Tor, an inland limestone cliff named after the hamlet at the western tip of Llanmadoc. Cwm Ivy has given its name to some woods, a marsh protected by a medieval seawall and a National Trust lodge. There used to be a field laboratory used by naturalists in the 1920s, but in 2011 the Cwm Ivy Lodge Bunkhouse (01792 390636) was opened here, used by volunteers and also by holidaymakers – a good, cheap alternative to a B&B if you want to spend the night in the area – see page 137.

Turn right here and go through a lever gate into a hillocky landscape. The WCP now makes a short, steep climb up a sandy track from 23 feet (7 metres) to 148 feet (45 metres) above sea level ⬛ᴄ. This is a kind of welcome to wild Gower, and you begin to see the landscape and views that won the peninsula its AONB status back in 1956. At the summit of this section, the headland of Hills Tor, you're only 154 feet (47 metres) above

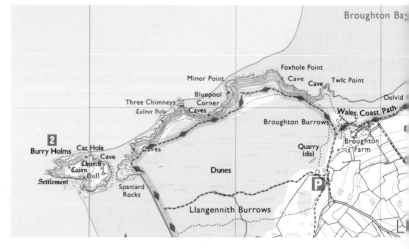

sea level, but you can see almost the whole of your coast walk since Amroth and beyond. Try to ignore the caravan sites as you take in the panoramic views.

The path, clearly and frequently waymarked from now on (WCP and Gower Coast Path signs), takes you along the tops of low cliffs, past the dunes of sweeping Broughton Bay and then climbing once again and out past Twic Point – the coast path veers to the right briefly here – and to Spaniard Rocks, allegedly named for a hoard of Spanish gold coins found after some long-forgotten shipwreck off the Gower coast.

If the tide is favourable, you can go all the way out to the small tidal island of Burry Holms **2** (from the Old Norse word *holmr* for islet). Archaeological evidence suggests this spot was 12 miles (19 km) inland in Mesolithic times (around 10,000 years ago). It's a pretty, grassy spot and in summer you may see white carnation-like sea campion and thrift, a pink-petalled coastal perennial.

After this you drop down to sea level for a lovely beach walk – Rhossili Bay is a stunner, and featured as the backdrop for a live broadcast of a choir singing 'Bread of Heaven' in the 2012 Olympic Games opening ceremony – and an easy low-level path along the west-facing bottom of Rhossili Down. At low tide you could obviously walk along the beach or, if you like views (and bracing winds), take the high-level path along the top of the hill, which is heathland covered in gorse, grass and heather. This way you get to set foot on the highest point on the Gower – the Beacon at 633 feet (193 metres) **3**. Whether you use the beach, the high road or the ordinary WCP, you will come out at a car park, close to the houses, restaurants, hotels and B&Bs of Rhossili.

A stay in Rhossili offers the opportunity to walk out to Worm's Head, one of the most dramatic and beautiful points on the Gower coast. See box, page 110.

Public transport

Rhossili (on route) 🚌
Llangenith (1 mile/1.6 km from route) 🚌

Refreshments and toilets

Llangennith (1 mile/1.6 km from route) King's Head
Rhossili (on route) Rhossili Visitor Centre Café ☕
Public toilets: Rhossili

Accommodation

Llangennith (1 mile/1.6 km from route) Hillend Caravan Park, Blas Gwyr, King's Head
Rhossili (on route) Worm's Head Hotel, Rhossili Bunkhouse (groups only during peak season)

Rhossili's wide beach and, behind it, Rhossili Down.

Whiteford Nature Reserve (Llanmadoc to Rhossili)

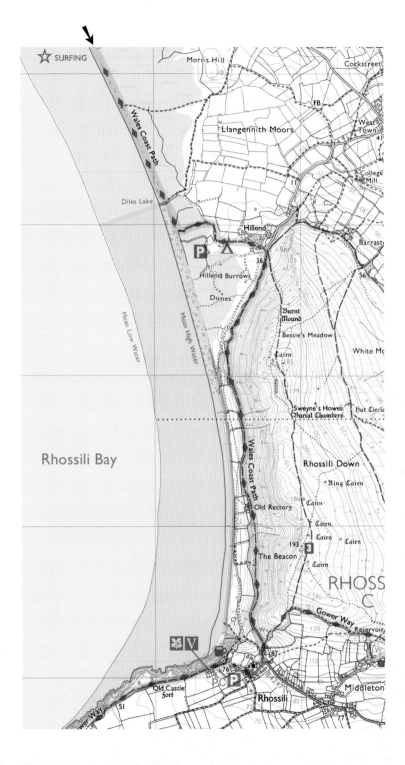

Morris Hill

Cockstreet

FB

Llangennith Moors

West Town

College Mill

Barrast

Diles Lake

Hillend

P ⛺

Spr

Hillend Burrows

36

Burnt Mound

Dunes

Bessie's Meadow

Cairn

White Mo

Sweyne's Howes Burial Chambers

Hut Circle

Rhossili Bay

Rhossili Down

Ring Cairn

Cairn

Wales Coast Path

Old Rectory

Cairn

Cairn Cairn

193

3

The Beacon

Cairn

RHOSS C

Gower Way

Reservoir

❀ V

PC P

Old Castle Fort

Rhossili

Middleton

Gower Way

Mean Low Water

Mean High Water

Worm's Head Walk

4.4 miles (7 km), low tide only

Allow two hours to do this side-walk up to the promontory of Worm's Head 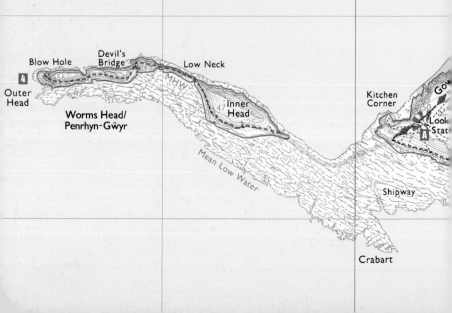 off Rhossili. It can only be done for 2½ hours on either side of low tide (making a 5-hour window), so make sure you plan your walk to coincide with this. You can get up-to-date information from the old coastguard lookout **A**, or by calling the coastguard on 01792 366534, or by checking the tide tables (see page 138).

The name Worm's Head comes from the Old Norse *wurm*, meaning 'dragon'. Viking marauders no doubt likened the promontory to a giant sea-serpent and gave it the evocative – and accidentally rather Welsh – name. The island is joined to the mainland by a rocky causeway and is made up of a large, flat-topped 'Inner Head', a 'Low Neck' leading across a natural rock bridge called Devil's Bridge and then the 'Outer Head'. The entire promontory is about a mile (1.6 km) long.

Starting at Rhossili car park, follow the path west for 0.8 mile (1.3 km) along the edge of the cliff till you pass the old coastguard's lookout. Here you'll be able to check on times (there will also be a sign giving the tide times a little further on).

From here it's a 0.7-mile (1.1-km) scramble across a causeway of jagged rocks to get to the grassy Inner Head. Regular visitors seem to find it easy to hop over the seaweed-strewn piles of shells, ponds, rocks and crevasses, and it pays to follow someone else so that you take the easiest route. Once you get to the promontory, if the wind is up walk on the low path to the left around the base of the hill. Alternatively, you can climb the hill and go westward that way (look out for seals on the rocks below here).

Devil's Bridge.

There's another long scramble here across a swathe of higher rocks and deeper chasms (the Low Neck) and then a short walk over a sea arch (Devil's Bridge) and then, after a very short rocky section, a final climb up to the top of the Outer Head. The summit is only around 157 feet (48 metres) above sea level, but the views back to South Gower, to Rhossili Bay and out to sea (you can see Tenby in the distance) are some of the best on the entire WCP.

The overall height gain for this short diversion is around 206 metres and you can rejoin the WCP either by retracing your steps or, on arrival at the coast beneath the coastguard station, following a lower path and then climbing up to the path just above Fall Bay.

The young Dylan Thomas made the fatal mistake of staying at Worm's Head after the tide had come in. He later wrote about his lonely fear stuck out on the rocks: 'I stayed on that Worm from dusk to midnight, sitting on that top grass, frightened to go further in because of the rats and because of things I am ashamed to be frightened of.' Between 21 March 2007 and 3 November 2012 a total of 47 people had to be rescued from Worm's Head.

Note that the Outer Head is closed from 1 March to 15 August (sometimes later) to protect nesting birds and their young.

Whiteford Nature Reserve (Llanmadoc) to Rhossili

Looking back over Rhossili Bay and south Gower from the tip of Worm's Head.

10 Rhossili to Oxwich

via Port Eynon and Horton

11.6 miles (18.7 km)

Ascent 1,299 feet (396 metres)
Highest point 360 feet (110 metres)

This section of the walk passes through one of the most dramatic landscapes of the WCP, as the route follows the cliff tops along several bays. The path is easy to follow and most of the detours to headlands and to the edges of the cliffs loop back to the main coast path. There are steep paths down to many of the beaches and bays; take care, as the descent is often more of a scramble than you might expect. There are quite a few sharp drops and climbs during the first 4 miles (6.4 km), but after this the path leads through more level pastoral land, then around Port Eynon drops to follow the line of the beach, before entering woodland close to Oxwich Bay. As you walk east, the coast of Somerset looks closer than ever and you can also see Lundy Island off the coast of Devon. Whether or not you make the trek out to Worm's Head (see box, page 110), where there's a seabird colony, you may see black-legged kittiwake, northern fulmar and European shag along the coast, and possibly gannets and Manx shearwater.

There are regular buses from Swansea Quadrant Bus Station to south Gower. Gower Explorer buses run every hour to Rhossili and Port Eynon (every two hours to Oxwich and Horton). There is also plenty of (paid) parking.

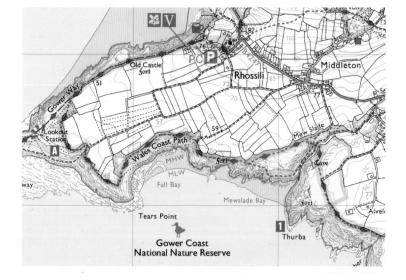

Old Castle Sort

Gower Way

51

Rhossili

Middleton

Lookout Station

A

Wales Coast Path

MHW

Sort

Mew Slade

Cave

MLW

Fall Bay

Mewslade Bay

Sort

Alvel

Tears Point

Gower Coast
National Nature Reserve

Thurba

1

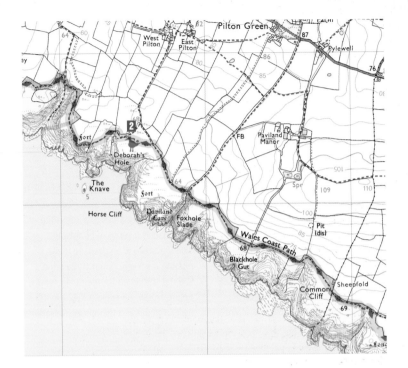

Look out for . . . Worm's Head, Thurba headland, The Knave, Deborah's Hole, Overton Cliff, Oxwich Wood

From Rhossili car park, take the tarmac path past the cottages, WCs and NT shop on the left, heading towards Worm's Head with Rhossili Bay to your right. Keeping the stone wall on your left, follow the grassy sward towards a small, stone building – the old coastguard lookout hut (now used by the National Coastwatch Institution, a voluntary organisation and registered charity that keeps watch over the causeway and helps walkers) **A**. Go left along a grassy path between gorse bushes until it meets a wall on the left.

After a few minutes you'll come to the wide, dramatic curve of Fall Bay and Mewslade Bay, where you can observe how the wave action has created sculptures from the limestone rock. What you see here

is the same strata of carboniferous limestone that drops beneath the sea at Stackpole Head in Pembrokeshire, only resurfacing here many miles to the east. The clean, white rock, made even more beautiful by the elements, in many ways defines south Gower.

The path now dips down a little before climbing to follow the top of the cliff edges, passing the prominent headlands of Thurba **1** and The Knave. It also passes close to Deborah's Hole **2**, a small nature reserve named after a bone cave (more of a pot-holer's cave, so hard to get deep inside). Ravens and fulmars have been seen nesting here, while the cave itself is known as a wintering refuge for greater horseshoe bats.

Rhossili to Oxwich

After about 1.5 miles (2.4 km) there's a right turn and a sharp drop for 5 minutes, followed by a slow climb back to cliff height. The path then goes up and down as it reaches each gully, and then levels out for a long stretch before the descent to the bottom of Overton cliff **3**.

As you continue around the headland, Port Eynon Point, make a tiny diversion to look inside Culver Hole **4**. This is a tall, narrow cave that houses a medieval dovecot (Old English *culufre* means pigeon or dove), and the holes where eggs were laid and the birds brooded are still visible. Shortly after the cave, back on the WCP, you'll pass the most southerly point on Gower and then see some nice new dragon-shell stone signage. Just before the village, there's a steep climb from sea level to about

98 feet (30 metres) and then scree and woods as you make the descent from Port Eynon Point to Port Eynon.

The WCP does not go directly down to the large ruin you see on the seafront (the old Salt House **5**, where sea water was boiled to extract salt), but turns left **B** then right to take you through a caravan site and on to the beach. Walk along the beach for 300 yards (280 metres), then turn left up a boardwalk to some snack bars. The path makes a right at The Seafarer, a fish and chip shop, then follows a series of boardwalks, sandy tracks and single-lane roads, passing a sewage pump station, the lifeboat station and some public toilets, before crossing a playing field (benches here) and passing the houses of Horton, the neighbouring village.

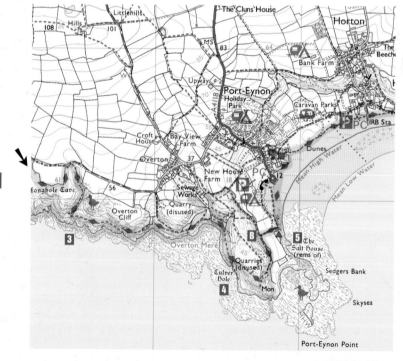

New stone signage on the approach to Port Eynon Point.

The sign reads:

Coast Path
Llwybr yr Arfordir

PORT EYNON ↑

Public footpath
Llwybr Troed

←

Port Eynon is thought to be named after an 11th-century Welsh prince who built a castle here, though there are no ruins (one legend is that the prince lived for a time as a hermit at Culver Hole). The village was once a booming centre for salting and for the oyster trade (the remains of oyster pools can be seen at low tide), limestone quarrying, lobstering and crabbing – and at one stage as many as eight excise officers were stationed here to deter smuggling.

Soon after Horton you are back on a rural coast path for the final hour's hike to Oxwich. The path runs close to the beach here, but there's still a low cliff, so take care. Shortly after a kissing-gate there's a longish diversion to avoid a section where the path has been eroded. Next comes grassland and signs up to Oxwich Green **C** – a slightly quicker route up to Oxwich if you're in a hurry or tired. The last half-hour of this walk is through Oxwich Wood – a dense swathe of ash, beech, oak and sycamore, with hart's-tongue fern and bluebells in the undergrowth during spring.

The woodland is pleasant and shady but does not extend the easiest of welcomes to Oxwich: you have to climb several steep sets of steps and then descend a similar number. It's quite a slog, but you'll eventually come down to a church and a road up to Oxwich Bay Hotel **D**.

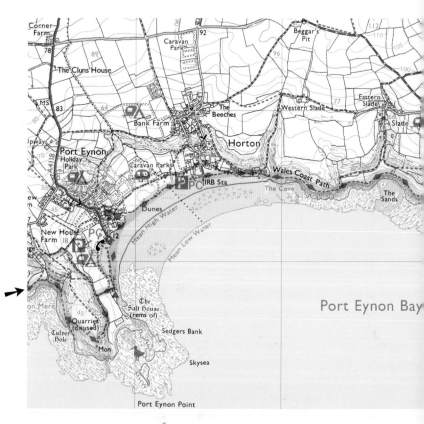

Public transport
Port Eynon (on route) 🚌
Oxwich (on route) 🚃

Refreshments and toilets
Port Eynon (on route) Smugglers Haunt
Oxwich (on route) Oxwich Bay Hotel
Fairyhill (4.6 miles/7.4 km inland)
Fairyhill Hotel and Restaurant
Food shops: Port Eynon, Oxwich
Public toilets: Port Eynon, Horton, Oxwich

Accommodation
Port Eynon (on route) Calver House
Hotel, Brook House B&B
Oxwich (on route) Little Haven Guest
House, Oxwich Bay Hotel
Fairyhill (4.6 miles/7.4 km inland)
Fairyhill Hotel

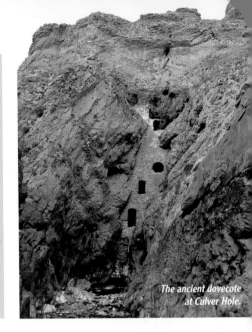

The ancient dovecote at Culver Hole.

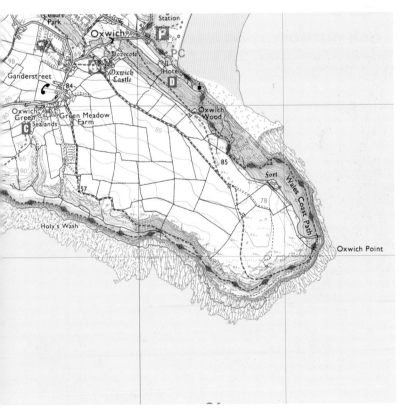

11 Oxwich to Caswell Bay

via Three Cliffs Bay and Pennard
8.7 miles (14.1 km)

Ascent 270 feet (82 metres)
Highest point 258 feet (77 metres)

This penultimate walk is full of visual treats, with several high cliffs and promontories and lots of accessible beaches and coves. Try to get a swim in at one of the beaches, and enjoy a picnic on one of the benches or in the café at Caswell Bay. As industrial Wales and its steaming chimneys begin to appear beyond the last few headlands, the Gower feels even more pristine and precious. Again, keep a lookout for birdlife – marine and terrestrial – all along this stretch.

There are regular buses from Swansea's Quadrant Bus Station into Oxwich, a small village that has a couple of shops, WCs, and food and drink at the hotel.

Look out for . . . Oxwich National Nature Reserve, Nicholaston Burrows, Three Cliffs Bay, Pennard Pill, Pwll Du Bay, Brandy Cove, Caswell Bay

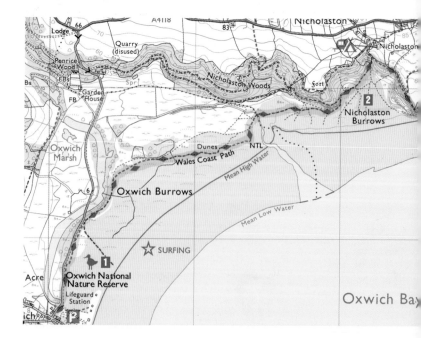

The first section takes you a little way along the road behind the Oxwich beach car park and then through the edge of the Oxwich National Nature Reserve **1**, where there are orchids, wooded cliffs and rare birds such as Cetti's warbler and bittern, as well as plenty of adders. The path runs along boardwalks and on narrow, sandy tracks, winding through dunes, slacks (dips between dunes) and salt marsh, before rising to the cliff top again around Nicholaston Burrows **2** – the beach and dunes tend to be a lot quieter at this end of the beach and there are great spots for a picnic and the opportunity for a quick swim.

After passing two headlands – Little Tor and the dramatic Great Tor – you will catch your first clear views of one of the Gower's most celebrated landmarks: Three Cliffs Bay, where the path veers inland to get around the freshwater river of Pennard Pill. In summer, if there's not been unusually heavy rain, you will probably be able to ford the pill, but during winter and after heavy rain it may be a couple of feet deep, in which case you have to follow the WCP signs to cross on stepping stones **A**. Note also that about 500 yards (450 metres) to the west of the pill is Pennard Castle **3**, a limestone and sandstone ruin dating from the 13th century.

The path now climbs again, returning to the cliff edge on a clearly marked path all the way round to Southgate **4**, a village to the south of – and contiguous with – Pennard. Here there are refreshments and a shop. You can either walk along a tarmac lane in front of the houses here or continue along the grass/stone paths to the right of it.

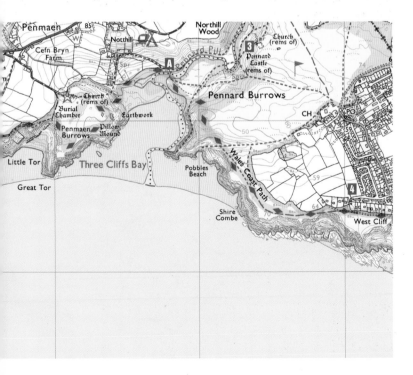

When the road curves left by a car park, go straight ahead across the grass and then, when the road rejoins from the left, either go along it or take the clifftop paths just to the right. The paths and road eventually converge as the housing on your left thins out and, at a bend in the road, you come to Hunts Farm.

Take the footpath signposted to the right, which descends and then ascends. Continue along the cliff top with the remains of a stone wall on your left. On the far side of Pwlldu Head **B**, the path – now going down – affords good views ahead of Pwlldu Bay and Caswell Bay and, in the distance, the smoking factories of Neath and Bridgend.

It's a steep descent to Pwlldu Bay **5**, where the path has to stay well to the left (north) of the beach because of a rushing river – if you want to cross to the shingle bank and get to the beach you'll see a path on the right. The sheltered bay here

was once a favoured location for smugglers, as they could keep a good lookout from the headland and could, when necessary, quickly vanish into the wooded valley and out of sight. Pwlldu Bay also served as a quarry until 1902, exporting limestone to north Devon. There were once five public houses here, but only two remain and sadly only as private houses – Ship Cottage (Ship Inn) and Beaufort House (Beaufort Arms). The National Trust owns the bay now.

It's a 10–15-minute walk along some lovely cliffs now to the next bay, Brandy Cove, where there's a bench if you need a rest. As the name suggests, this quiet little bay was used to unload illegal alcohol – and tobacco – during the 18th century. Small boats also used to load ore here from the lead mines that were once worked nearby. Brandy Cove is associated with a couple of supernatural legends. One tells of a witch called Old Moll, whose screams the locals said they often heard

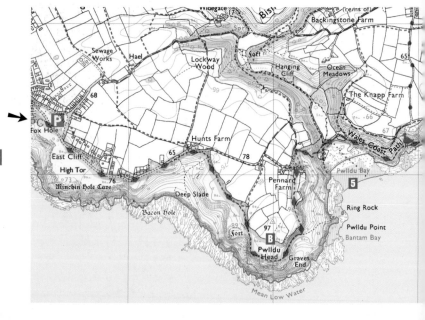

Looking west from Pwlldu Head.

coming from the caves at night. Then, in 1961, three pot-holers found an old skeleton in a disused lead mine here. Upon examination, it was found to have been cut into three pieces. As the police trawled through their old missing persons' files, the name of Mamie Stuart, an attractive chorus girl who had disappeared suddenly in 1919, came to their attention. Her husband was suspected of the crime but had died three years before the discovery was made.

A short climb takes you above Brandy Cove and round a shallow headland into Caswell Bay. There's a high-tide route here along the road, but the low-tide one takes you down to the beach in front of an apartment block and then across the sand to the Surfstyle Café **C**, which serves cakes, sandwiches and other refreshments. Caswell Bay is popular with surfers and often has gentle waves ideal for those trying to learn to surf. There are WCs above the beach, in the car park.

Public transport
Three Cliffs Bay (on route) 🚌
Pennard/Southgate (on route) 🚌
Caswell Bay (on route) 🚌

Refreshments and toilets
Caswell Bay (on route) Surf Side Café 🥄
Public toilets: Southgate, Caswell Bay

Accommodation
Pennard (on route) self-catering cottages
Three Cliffs Bay (on route) Lavender Cottage

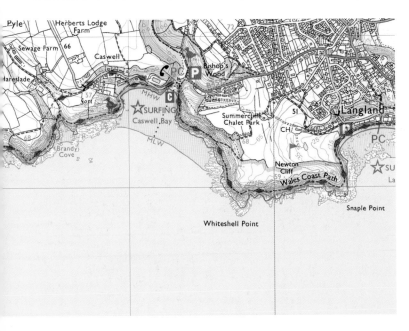

12 Caswell Bay to Swansea (Abertawe)

via Langland and Mumbles
9.1 miles (14.7 km)

Ascent 362 feet (110 metres)
Highest point 230 feet (70 metres)

With its sandy beach, the resort is popular with families and there's a lifeguard on duty in summer. When the wind is up, surfers gather here but at other times there's good swimming and the beach often wins a Blue Flag.

Caswell Bay is served by regular buses from Swansea bus station and from Mumbles (10 minutes away by road). There are regular buses between Mumbles and Swansea in case you want to end your walk at Mumbles.

Look out for . . . Langland Bay, Mumbles Pier, 5 Cwmdonkin Drive and the Dylan Thomas Centre at Swansea

This last section takes you out of rural Gower and into urban Wales, via the sweeping promenade that links Mumbles to Swansea. Unless you absolutely love

cities, you may prefer to break your journey at the former, spend the night there and then continue to Swansea, see a few sights, then jump on a train or bus

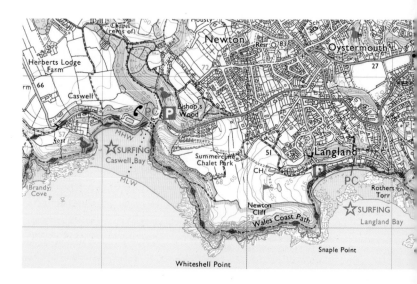

to go home. Mumbles is quieter and prettier and has plenty of pubs and bars, shops, small supermarkets, restaurants, hotels and B&Bs.

The path climbs again after Caswell and goes back out to the cliff edge, towards Whiteshell Point and Snaple Point, skirting around a golf course, and then crosses another surfing and swimming beach, Langland, which is at the edge of the conurbation of The Mumbles. The WCP from here follows a lower, but still beautiful, coastal route all the way to Limeslade Bay, where the path joins the road **A**. As you approach the corner you will see, on your right-hand side, Bracelet Bay and Mumbles Head — with its lighthouse **1** — and then the pier, at which point you will suddenly sense you've arrived in the outskirts of a city.

The Mumbles — which may get its name from the sound of the sea on the rocks, or from the silhouette of the islands and headlands, which look a bit like *mamillae* (Latin for breasts) — was an oyster-harvesting and fishing village on the west of Swansea Bay from Roman times until the 18th century. In 1807 a railroad carriage was converted to be pulled by a horse in order to carry people here from Swansea. As the latter's dockside became busier and dirtier, the beach at The Mumbles (often called simply Mumbles, without the definite article) grew in popularity.

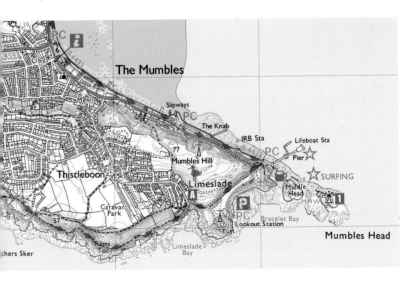

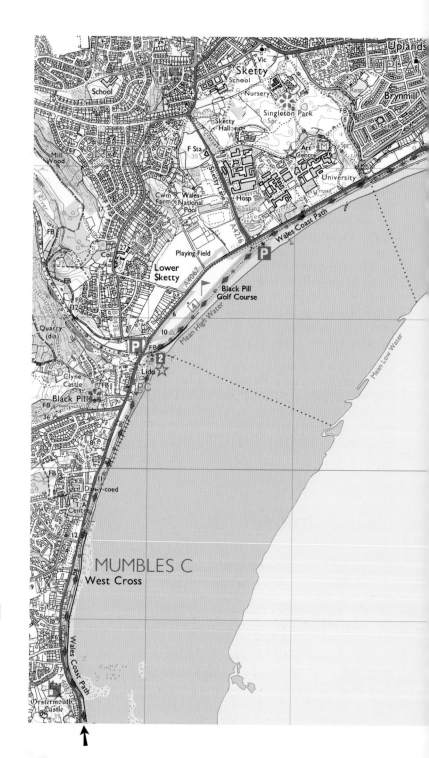

The WCP follows the promenade all the way to the Maritime Quarter in Swansea (Abertawe), passing through West Cross and Black Pill Bay **2** (where there's a good café-restaurant called The Junction), past the university campus and along the southern edge of Uplands, the area associated with Dylan Thomas. The WCP goes along the wharf across from the National Waterfront Museum **3**. The walk, for the purposes of this book, ends on the coast at the Marina Towers Observatory (aka the Tower of the Ecliptic) **4**, built in 1988 and, closed since 2009, due to re-open as a café-bar and holiday apartment. From here it's a 10-minute walk to Swansea city centre and 15 minutes to the railway station.

If Swansea doesn't look very pretty, bear in mind that it was flattened during the Second World War. The so-called Swansea Blitz took place from 19 to 21 February 1941, when incendiary bombs and high explosives were dropped on the town centre – on the 21st the raid started late in the evening and lasted for five hours. Hundreds of residents were killed or injured and the glow of the fires was seen 75 miles (120 km) away in Fishguard. The Maritime

Quarter has been revamped successively – if not altogether successfully – over the last few decades and the National Waterfront Museum is definitely worth a look. If you have an hour or two to spare, you could also try to visit the Dylan Thomas Centre and the Glyn Vivian Art Gallery to see something of Swansea's artistic side.

For a fuller account of Swansea's glories, see box, page 133.

Public transport
Langland Bay (on route) 🚌
Mumbles (on route) 🚌
Swansea (on route) ≅, 🚌

Refreshments and toilets
Mumbles (on route) Kitchen Table, Café 93 ☕
Black Pill (on route) Junction Café ☕
Swansea (on route) Wide selection
Food shops: Mumbles, Swansea
Public toilets: Mumbles, Black Pill Lido, Swansea

Accommodation
Mumbles (on route) Langland Road B&B, Patrick With Rooms, Tides Reach Guest House
Swansea (on route) Wide selection

Caswell Bay to Swansea

Dylan Thomas

Poet of the 'heron-priested shore'

Dylan Thomas called Swansea, his birthplace, an 'ugly, lovely town'. He called Laugharne, where he is buried, a 'legendary lazy little black magical bedlam by the sea'. There's ambivalence beneath the humour in the descriptions. Still, the tourist boards in both places like to claim the poet as their own, and little wonder, given his prominence in 20th-century poetry – and his pulling power.

Though Dylan Thomas travelled widely as an adult, and spent many a happy hour in London and New York, the landscapes and people of his youth and his homeland provided much raw material for his best work. Visitors to the coastal towns linked to his name and to the rural hinterland between them will find their experience enriched if they pack a copy of the poetry as well as this guide. Biographies by Andrew Lycett and Paul Ferris, and Thomas's wife's memoir, *Caitlin: Life with Dylan Thomas – A Warring Absence* (the title says it all), will fill in all the gaps about his life. But if you've not time for those, here's a potted poet's life to think on as you walk . . .

The life

Dylan Marlais Thomas was born on 27 October 1914 at 5 Cwmdonkin Drive, a newly built semi-detached house in the Uplands area of Swansea. The name Dylan was at the time not common at all – his father took it from the medieval Welsh classic, the *Mabinogion*. His parents, Florence and David John (known as DJ), spoke Welsh but brought up their children to speak only English. Uplands was an anglicised area and many other middle-class children born to Welsh-speakers in the area were brought up speaking only English.

Both parents read to the young Dylan and in January 1927 he sold a poem, 'His Requiem', to the *Western Mail* newspaper in Cardiff. After leaving school, he worked as a reporter for the *South Wales Evening Post* and from 1933 onwards his poetry began to get attention. A submission to the BBC was read on air.

In 1936, Dylan met Caitlin Macnamara in a pub in Fitzrovia, London. They fell in love and married but their relationship was tainted by infidelity as well as by money worries and Dylan's drinking habits. In spring 1938, the family moved to Laugharne, living first in a cottage called Eros in Gosport Street and then at a house called Sea View. Their first child, Llewellyn, was born in January 1939.

Laugharne inspired some of Thomas's finest poetry and prose. The adolescent adventures featured in *A Portrait of the Artist as a Young Dog* were edited in the castle gazebo, which was owned by the novelist Richard Hughes (*A High Wind in Jamaica*). The poems 'Over Sir John's Hill', 'Do Not Go Gentle' and 'Poem On His Birthday' were written in Laugharne, and it was here he gathered most of the material for his most famous work, *Under Milk Wood*, listening to stories whilst sitting in the kitchen and bar at Brown's Hotel.

Other poems celebrate other parts of south and west Wales, including 'Fern Hill' (1945) which evokes childhood memories from time spent at his Aunt Annie's farm, Fernhill, just outside Llangain in Carmarthenshire.

In early 1949 the house which was to become the Thomas family home, The Boathouse, came on the market for £3,000. The historian A. J. P. Taylor's wife, Margaret, who had long been a patron, bought it and the Thomases moved in. Caitlin gave birth to a son, Colm, in July of that year.

In 1950 Dylan embarked on a lengthy tour of the USA to earn some money. In his absence Caitlin began to feel suffocated by Laugharne. When he returned from America they had drunken rows which occasionally became violent on both sides. Thomas made two further trips to America and in October 1953 made a fourth – and final – visit. On 3 November he attended a party, but returned early to his hotel. Unable to sleep, he left his room for a drink. The next morning he was taken to St Vincent's Hospital where he lapsed into a coma for five days, dying on 9 November 1953. Caitlin later wrote, 'Dylan had this rather odd view that all the best poets died young and that he himself would never make forty, and there were times when he almost seemed to live his life by that'.

The work

Talented people who die young usually find their biographies overshadow their work. When he's not being compared with T. S. Eliot and W. B. Yeats, Dylan Thomas is often caricatured as a boozing second-rate pseudo-poet (a sort of ugly Jim Morrison), as a romantic hero (a latter-day Keats) or as a Welsh one-off (a precursor to Richey Edwards of the Manic Street Preachers).

Perhaps because of their showy wordsmithery, Thomas's poems have been described as 'intellectual fakes of the highest class'. Even fans accept that his output was uneven. But from his earliest volume, *Eighteen Poems* (1934), he was considered relevant enough to be reviewed in the *Times Literary Supplement* and *Spectator*. In the then influential *Time and Tide*, one critic remarked, 'This is not merely a book of unusual promise; it is more probably the sort of bomb that bursts not more than once in three years.'

Thomas was obsessed with words – with their sound but also with their ambiguity, and it is the latter that gives many of his poems their inherent difficulty. He exploited the speech-like qualities of 'sprung rhythm' to arguably greater effect than its innovator, Gerard Manley Hopkins, experimented with internal rhyme and alliteration, and re-ordered syntax in a revolutionary manner, and his use of cosmic and sexual imagery shows a mind struggling with ideas as well as

Dylan Thomas's birthplace: 5 Cwmdonkin Drive in Uplands, Swansea.

The Boathouse and the Tâf at low tide.

personal issues. Thomas recognized 'immature violence' and 'incoherence' in his own work, and was embarrassed to admit his poems sometimes veered towards surrealism and exuded heady whiffs of pretension and obscurantism.

But in his 1936 collection, *Twenty-five Poems*, poems such as 'This Bread I Break', 'The Hand That Signed the Paper', and 'And Death Shall Have No Dominion' reveal that Thomas could achieve greater impact by delivering his ideas in a straightforward, even strident manner.

The 1946 poetry collection, *Deaths and Entrances,* contains many of his most famous poems, including 'A Refusal to Mourn the Death, by Fire, of a Child in London', 'Poem in October', 'The Hunchback in the Park' and 'Fern Hill'. A pastoral mood comes to the fore, but metaphysical themes like time and death are never far from the vision here and some critics have noted a new, 'sacramental' concept of the natural world. His flair for rhythm – at their best his verses flow with a sort of natural, organic breeziness – is now placed at the service of

his mature thought processes and yet, still, his ability to surprise with stirring turns of phrase is in evidence. The closing image of 'Fern Hill' – 'Time held me green and dying / Though I sang in my chains like the sea' – is as pithy and powerful as anything in 20th-century poetry.

Dylan Thomas's legacy is everywhere, and growing. In Laugharne, there's the Dylan Thomas Birthday Walk, a house-museum (The Boathouse), a hotel-and-pub full of his books (Brown's) and a white cross marking the grave he shares with Caitlin. Swansea has a full-blown Dylan Thomas Centre showcasing his writings alongside photographs and memorabilia, and 5 Cwmdonkin Drive is also open to the public for guided tours, events and as a four-room self-catering guesthouse.

In 2014, to commemorate the centenary of his birth, Laugharne and Swansea and other towns and villages associated with his life and work are hosting events and shows and walks aimed at rediscovering his writing – and attracting tourists, of course. See www.dt100.info for details.

The grave of Dylan and Caitlin Thomas in the overspill cemetery at St Martin's Church, Laugharne.

Swansea

The rise and fall of a second city

In an update of Dylan Thomas's oft-quoted remark that Swansea was an 'ugly, lovely town', corrupt cop Terry Walsh (played by Dougray Scott), in the 1997 film *Twin Town*, describes Swansea as a 'pretty shitty city'.

Most Cardiffians would agree, and even outside Swansea's great rival, few sober Welsh men and women would venture that Wales's second city was an attractive place. For shopping, for leisure, for culture and for cuisine, many locals speed on to the M4 to go east to the renascent capital, while tourists tend to bypass the urban sprawl – 239,000 people live in and around the city – to go west to Mumbles and the Gower Peninsula.

At first glance Swansea has a striking topography, a bit like Rio de Janeiro flattened and then placed under a cloud that drizzles year round. In place of the *favelas* are the identikit terraced houses ranked along steep-sided hills. Poverty and desolation are everywhere. Boy racers cane their electric-blue Subarus into the grey suburbs. Only sweeping Swansea Bay – the Guanabara of Glamorgan – offers some solace to the eye.

The reasons for the urban blight are many. A key factor was the Blitz, which obliterated, along with lives and livelihoods, much of the past. But Swansea has one . . .

The name of the city has nothing to do with swans or sea. It was once called *Sweins eg* or *ey*, Swein's Island, which purportedly stood in the mouth of the River Tawe – the Welsh name is Abertawe.

Who Swein was is not known, but he may have been a Norseman who built a fort on the island around AD 1,000 as a base for raiding the Welsh coast.

The town was founded in the early 12th century during the Norman conquest of Wales. A wooden castle was constructed on what is now Worcester Place, rebuilt in stone in the early 13th century – and still visible at the southern end of High Street, somewhat lost among modern buildings.

A town, with market and garrison, grew up around the castle. Many of the townspeople were English immigrants and at some time between 1158 and 1184 Swansea was granted a charter. King John then gave it a second, royal charter in 1215, permitting trade, and the city began to export hides, wool, butter, cheese and grain to England.

Swansea grew around coal mining and iron ore extraction, shipbuilding and shipping, and in the late 18th century saw booms in copper, lead and pottery. In the 19th century zinc and tinplate (steel covered in tin) turned the city into a metalworking powerhouse, and the already bustling port had to expand. North Dock was built in 1852, South Dock in 1859 and in 1881 the Prince of Wales Dock was built on the east bank of the Tawe. In 1801 the population was around 6,800; by the end of the century it had passed 100,000. During the last three decades, the docks have been redeveloped – and rebranded as the 'Maritime Quarter' (or 'Marina') – but a walk around the still waters of the wharves evokes the ghosts of Swansea's seafaring past.

The Second World War (see page 127), combined with the depletion of native ores, global and national recessions and depressions, underinvestment and foreign competition, ended Swansea's long history of industrial growth. By the time Prince Charles made it a city to mark his investiture, it seemed more of a token gesture than a formal recognition. In 1997 Swansea City Council's proposal for the Welsh National Assembly to be housed in the Guildhall was rejected in favour of the new Senedd building in Cardiff. Instead, the city was gifted the £33.5 million National Waterfront Museum – a memorial to the industrial revolution in Wales. The latter is an impressive structure and Swansea needs more of them: its post-war buildings are among the grimmest in the UK and its town planning among the most oxymoronic (or just plain moronic) in Western Europe.

Press and public seem to enjoy putting Swansea down. A local newspaper reported that High Street was the 'worst entrance to a city centre'; the *Daily Telegraph* did a slideshow showing Swansea as one of the 'worst ten cities for youth'. Online yappers get stuck in too. 'Swansea is the only place outside of Arkansas and Turkmenistan where having a mullet is considered cool,'

writes one, awarding the city the title of 'the steroid abuse capital of Europe.'

Despite the urban decay and bad press, Swansea has strengths. Some of these are enduring, others probably ephemeral: the thriving Premiership football club; the successes of the Ospreys regional rugby union club (in 2006 it beat Australia 24–16, becoming the first and, to date, only Welsh regional team to triumph against a major touring side). Swansea also has a place in cricket legend, as its picturesque St Helens ground (also used for rugby) was where Garry Sobers hit his six 6s. Then there are the two universities, the DVLA (which employs around 5,000 staff in Swansea) and both the Welsh-language and English-language literary heritage: Dylan Thomas, Vernon Watkins, Kingsley Amis (his 1954 novel *Lucky Jim* satirised Swansea University's academic establishment; 32 years later, *The Old Devils* lampooned its middle classes).

Trainspotters and history buffs get misty-eyed about the Swansea and Mumbles Railway, which opened on 25 March 1807 to carry coal and limestone, and later on became the first train in the world to carry paying passengers; a replica of the first horse-drawn carriage is on display in the tram shed in the Marina. For locals there are many keenly loved icons – some extant, some phantasmal: the No Sign Bar (the city's oldest wine bar); the Tower of the Ecliptic astronomical observatory (soon to become a café-bar), built in 1991; the gracious Morgan's Hotel; the magnificently (mis)named Salubrious Passage off Wind Street; the Old Carlton Cinema (now a bookshop) . . .

But Swansea's qualities may be more oblique and also more precious. In the

The Swansea and Mumbles Railway, the world's first paying passenger service.

Historic ships at the National Waterfront Museum, Swansea.

richly detailed *Real Swansea*, poet and university lecturer Nigel Jenkins writes: 'If the architectural banality of the city centre is an ever-present reminder of the Blitz, it can't be said that the war did lasting damage to the Swansea spirit, which is as spry and resourceful as ever'. There is something in the size and breeziness and energy of the city that works, and works well at the human level, for all the dysfunction in other quarters. Surrounded by farmland and caravan sites, not far from the sad valleys and redundant industrial towns, Swansea has nonetheless retained a cosmopolitan brio, and is confident and muscular in the same way as Manchester and Birmingham are in England. But, as Jenkins notes, the key for Swansea is to 'stop looking edgily over its shoulder'. If ever there was a metropolis with second-city syndrome, it's Wales's western gateway and maybe the clue is there in that compass point: Swansea should look inland, westward, facing the rest of Wales, and find its future there.

Pay homage to . . .

Swansea Jack – a black retriever who worked in the docks in the thirties and is said to have rescued 27 people from drowning; there's a monument on the seafront opposite the St Helen's cricket ground in Brynmill and a pub honouring the dog's memory on Oystermouth Road.

The Kardomah Gang – a group of thirties would-be bohemians that included poets Dylan Thomas, Vernon Watkins, Charles Fisher and John Prichard, artists Alfred Janes and Mervyn Levy, composer and linguist Daniel Jones. The Kardomah café is on Portland Street – not the original (that was on Castle Street), but still a lovely combination of fifties-style greasy spoon and 21st-century retro chic, grinding its own beans.

Dylan Thomas – visit 5 Cwmdonkin Drive where he was born, in Uplands, 1.5 miles (2.4 km) west of the city centre, and the Dylan Thomas Centre close to the Marina. The latter has a Swansea city Dylan-themed walk on its website.

Useful Information

Contact details

This section includes details of telephone numbers, websites and email addresses where available. If no email address is shown, it may be possible to send an email via the website.

Official Wales Coast Path
ⓘ www.walescoastpath.gov.uk
✉ enquiries@ccw.gov.uk

The 'static maps' on this site are particularly useful if you want to study the WCP online.

Visit Wales Contact Centre
ⓘ www.visitwales.co.uk/
✉ info@visitwales.co.uk
☎ 08708 300306 or 08708 300306
Opening hours: 9am–5pm Mon–Fri, except for Christmas Day, Boxing Day and New Year's Day.

Carmarthenshire County Council
Carmarthenshire County Council, County Hall, Carmarthen SA31 1JP
ⓘ www.carmarthenshire.gov.uk/
✉ direct@carmarthenshire.gov.uk
☎ 01267 234567

Ceredigion County Council
Canolfan Rheidol, Rhodfa Padarn, Llanbadarn Fawr, Aberystwyth, Ceredigion SY23 3UE
ⓘ www.ceredigion.gov.uk/
✉ reception@ceredigion.gov.uk
☎ 01545 570881

Countryside Council for Wales
ⓘ www.ccw.gov.uk
☎ 0845 1306 229

Pembrokeshire Coast Path
ⓘ nt.pcnpa.org.uk/

Pembrokeshire County Council
County Hall, Haverfordwest SA61 1TP
ⓘ www.pembrokeshire.gov.uk/
☎ 01437 764551

Pendine Sands
Pendine Community Council
ⓘ www.pendinesands.org/
☎ 01994 427019

Swansea County Council
Civic Centre, Oystermouth Road, Swansea SA1 3SN
ⓘ www.swansea.gov.uk/
☎ 01792 636000

Travel information

There are daily rail services between Carmarthenshire – though not the coast – and the rest of Wales and regular trains to Manchester. The hub is Carmarthen and there are also trains from Ferryside and Kidwelly (on request). Llanelli has frequent services to Swansea and Cardiff.

Swansea has regular services to Cardiff, Bristol, London and Manchester. The Heart of Wales line links both Llanelli and Swansea to Shrewsbury and rural Carmarthenshire and Powys.

Trains from Pembroke and Fishguard connect with ferries from Rosslare in Ireland.

Rail

National Rail Enquiries
ⓘ hwww.nationalrail.co.uk/
☎ National Rail Enquiries: 08457 48 49 50
(TrainTracker automated service on 0871 200 49 50)

Traveline
ⓘ www.traveline-cymru.info/
☎ 0871 200 22 33

Arriva Trains
ⓘ www.arrivatrainswales.co.uk/home.aspx
☎ 08457 48 49 50
(24-hour National Rail Enquiries line)
0845 60 40 500 (National Rail Enquiries Welsh Language Service)

First Group
ⓘ www.firstgroup.com/ukbus/south_west_wales/
☎ 08457 48 49 50
(24-hour National Rail Enquiries line)
☎ 0871 200 2233 (bus enquiries)

The Heart of Wales Line
ⓘ www.heart-of-wales.co.uk/
☎ 01597 822053

Coach and bus

There are daily, direct National Express services from London to Carmarthen (the fastest daily service leaves at midday taking 5 hours 35 minutes) and Swansea (4 hours 35 minutes).

The main towns – Llanelli, St Clears and Burry Port – are well connected to Carmarthen and Swansea. The latter's Quadrant Bus Station is the regional hub. Services to the smaller coastal towns and villages are infrequent and often limited to daylight hours.

For long-distance bus services use www.trawscymru.info

National Express Coaches
ⓘ www.nationalexpress.com/home.aspx
☎ 0871 200 2233

Carmarthenshire bus timetables
ⓘ www.carmarthenshire.gov.uk/english/transport/buses/pages/bustimetables.aspx

Swansea
For buses use www.traveline-cymru.info
A special Sunday Explorer bus runs between Swansea and Rhossili on Sundays and Bank Holidays; see
ⓘ http://visitswanseabay.com/explorebybus for all timetables.

Accommodation

There are B&Bs in all the villages and small towns on this section of the Wales Coast Path, and static caravans and chalets in many areas too. There are hotels in Swansea, Llanelli and Carmarthen and in the bigger villages and townships, such as Laugharne and Ferryside.

It's easy to browse and book accommodation online, but if you plan on doing your walk between June and September, book well in advance. The regional tourist information centres will be able to advise on proximity and to give you a list of hotels in any particular town or village.

Visit Wales
ⓘ www.visitwales.co.uk/holiday-accommodation-in-wales/

Stay in Wales
ⓘ www.stayinwales.co.uk/
☎ 02921 251009

Youth hostels

Youth Hostel Association
ⓘ www.yha.org.uk
✉ customerservices@yha.org.uk
☎ 0800 0191700 / 01629 592700
8am–8pm (Mon–Fri), 9am–5pm (Sat)
There are no YHA youth hostels in Carmarthenshire, but there are four on the Gower Peninsula.

Gower Bunkhouse
Borfa House Activity Centre, Port Eynon, Swansea SA3 1NN
☎ 01792 401548

Port Eynon
Old Lifeboat House, Port Eynon, Swansea SA3 1NN
☎ 0845 371 9135

Rhossili Bunkhouse
Rhossili Activity Centre, Middleton, Rhossili, Swansea SA3 1PL – groups only during peak season
ⓘ www.rhossilibunkhouse.com/default/index.php
☎ 01792 401548

Swansea Bunkhouse (groups only)
Dan-y-Coed House, Huntington Close, West Cross, Swansea SA3 5AL
☎ 01792 401548
The National Trust has good-value accommodation near Llanmadoc and Whiteford Point; the Cwm Ivy Lodge Bunkhouse sleeps 10 and costs just £130 per night Mon–Thurs, £150 per night Fri–Sun.
ⓘ www.nationaltrust.org.uk/gower or see
ⓘ www.facebook.com/GowerNT
✉ kimberley.boland@nationaltrust.org.uk
☎ 01792 390636

See www.independenthostelguide.co.uk for non-affiliated youth hostels.
The following websites may also be of use:

ⓘ www.rarebits.co.uk/home

ⓘ www.walescottages.co.uk

ⓘ www.fbmholidays.co.uk

ⓘ www.qualitycottages.co.uk/index.php

ⓘ www.coastalwales.co.uk

Tourist information

Information Wales
ⓘ www.wales.info/
✉ tourism@wales.info

Discover Carmarthenshire
Old Castle House, adjacent to County Hall, Carmarthen, Carmarthenshire SA31 1JP
ⓘ www.discovercarmarthenshire.com/index.html
☎ 01267 231557

Discover Gower
ⓘ www.discovergower.com/
☎ 01792 360624

Enjoy Gower
ⓘ www.enjoygower.com
✉ info@mumblestic.co.uk
☎ 01792 361302

Millennium Coastal Park
Discovery Centre, North Dock, Llanelli, Carmarthenshire SA15 2LF
ⓘ www.millenniumcoastalpark.com/
☎ 01554 777744

Mumbles Tourist Information Centre
Mumbles Methodist Church, 520B Mumbles Road, Mumbles, Swansea SA3 4DH
ⓘ www.mumblesinfo.org.uk/
✉ info@mumblestic.co.uk
☎ 01792 361302

Tenby Tourist Information Centre
Unit 2, Upper Park Road, Tenby SA70 7LT
ⓘ www.pembrokeshire.gov.uk/
✉ tenby.tic@pembrokeshire.gov.uk
☎ 01834 842402

Visit Swansea
Plymouth Street (back of Grand Theatre), Swansea SA1 3QG
ⓘ www.visitswanseabay.com
✉ tourism@swansea.gov.uk
☎ 01792 468321

Tide tables
For times of high and low tides along the route, see www.tidetimes.org.uk

Museums and tourist attractions

Dylan Thomas Birthplace
5 Cwmdonkin Drive, Uplands, Swansea SA2 0RA
ⓘ www.5cwmdonkindrive.com
✉ info@dylanthomasbirthplace.com
☎ 01792 472555

Dylan Thomas Boathouse at Laugharne
Dylan Thomas Boathouse, Dylan's Walk, Laugharne SA33 4SD
ⓘ www.dylanthomasboathouse.com/
✉ boathouse@carmarthenshire.gov.uk
☎ 01994 427420
Open May–October and Easter weekend 10am–5.30pm (last admission 5.00pm); November to April 10.30am–3.30pm (last admission 3.00pm)

Dylan Thomas Centre
Somerset Place, Swansea SA1 1RR
ⓘ www.dylanthomas.com/
✉ dylanthomas.lit@swansea.gov.uk
☎ 01792 463980

Fairyhill
Reynoldston, Gower, Swansea SA3 1BS
ⓘ www.fairyhill.net
☎ 01792 390139

Gower Heritage Centre
Parkmill, Swansea SA3 2EH
ⓘ www.gowerheritagecentre.co.uk
✉ reception@gowerheritagecentre.co.uk
☎ 01792 371206

Museum of Speed (open summer only)
Pendine, Carmarthenshire SA33 4NY
ⓘ www.carmarthenshire.gov.uk/english/education/museums/museumofspeed
✉ museums@carmarthenshire.gov.uk
☎ 01994 453488 (Easter–September)
☎ 01267 228696 (October–Easter)

National Garden Scheme
Delacorse, Laugharne, Carmarthenshire, Carmarthenshire & Pembrokeshire SA33 4QP
ⓘ www.ngs.org.uk/
✉ annie.hart@ymail.com
☎ 01994 427728

Parc Le Breos
Parkmill, Gower, Swansea SA3 2HA
ⓘ www.parc-le-breos.co.uk
✉ info@parclebreos.co.uk
☎ 01792 371636

Pennard Castle
Three Cliffs Bay, Gower, Swansea
ⓘ www.castlewales.com/pennard

Local organisations

In addition to the bodies listed above that deal specifically with tourism matters, there are a number of local organisations that contribute to the protection or management of the Welsh coast and its wildlife. They all have a role to play, not least in informing and educating the public on matters relating to the coastal environment. They need members and they need financial resources to enable them to act effectively in the protection of vulnerable sites and the encouragement of responsible visitor use.

Gower Society
Swansea Museum, Victoria Road, Swansea
SA1 3SN
ⓘ www.the gowersociety.org.uk
✉ contact@thegowersociety.org.uk

National Coastwatch Institution
National Office, Unit 25, Basepoint Business Centre, Yeoford Way, Exeter, Devon EX2 8LB
ⓘ www.nci.org.uk/links
☎ 0300 111 1202

National Trust (Wales)
Ymddiriedolaeth Genedlaethol, National Trust, Trinity Square, Llandudno, Conwy LL30 2DE
ⓘ www.nationaltrust.org.uk/visit/local-to-you/wales/
✉ wa.customerenquiries@nationaltrust.org.uk
☎ 01492 860 123

Royal Society for the Protection of Birds
RSPB Cymru, Sutherland House, Castlebridge, Cowbridge Road East, Cardiff CF11 9AB
ⓘ www.rspb.org.uk/wales/
✉ cymru@rspb.org.uk
☎ 029 2035 3000,

Wetland and Wildfowl Trust/National Wetland Centre
WWT National Wetland Centre Wales
Llwynhendy, Llanelli, Carmarthenshire
SA14 9SH
ⓘ www.wwt.org.uk/visit/llanelli/
✉ info.llanelli@wwt.org.uk
☎ 01554 741087

Woodland Trust Wales (Coed Cadw)
The Woodland Trust Wales (Coed Cadw), 3 Cooper's Yard, Curran Road, Cardiff CF10 5NB
ⓘ www.woodlandtrust.org.uk
✉ info@coed-cadw.org.uk
☎ 08452 935860

Nearby places of interest

This guide has limited itself to the coast and a short distance inland, where a castle or other sight is worth a slight detour. But Carmarthenshire and Swansea Bay have natural, cultural and historical attractions away from the coast and the following is a list of just four inland sites worth considering as additions to your walking holiday. They are listed west to east.

National Botanic Garden of Wales
In Llanarthne, 8 miles east of Carmarthen, this impressive 560-acre site has splendid themed gardens and boasts around 8,000 different plant varieties. It is home to the world's largest single-spanned glasshouse, designed by Lord Foster, which houses the most comprehensive display of Mediterranean climate-zone plants in the northern hemisphere. Take the 166 bus from Carmarthen and you get half-price entry.
ⓘ www.gardenofwales.org.uk

Dinefwr Park and Castle
This National Trust property comprises a 12th-century Welsh castle, historic house and 18th-century landscape park, enclosing a medieval deer park. The railway station at Llandeilo, a pretty inland town, is a mile away, and there are buses if you don't fancy the walk.
ⓘ www.nationaltrust.org.uk/dinefwr/

Carreg Cennen Castle

Spectacularly positioned on a limestone cliff, 14th-century Carreg Cennen is often described as Wales's most romantic castle. Managed by Cadw (the Welsh Assembly's heritage arm), it is located close to Llandeilo.
ⓘ www.carregcennencastle.com

Brecon Beacons

If the coast walk has been a little too gentle, you could head inland to the Black Mountain range (Y Mynydd Du), in the western fringes of the Brecon Beacons National Park. The Forest Fawr Geopark has some good hill-climbing.
ⓘ www.breconbeacons.org

Bibliography

Carmarthenshire and Swansea Bay support an army of local historians and nature lovers and the Welsh coast has inspired a lot of great writing. The following is a short selection of useful guides, background books and lyrical works.

Allen, K., and Durden, P., *Twin Town* (ScreenPress, 1997)
Avery, G., *Gower Coastal Walks* (D. W. Jones, 2001)
Hughes, W., *Carmarthen: History and Celebration* (Francis Frith, 2011)
Jenkins, N., *Circular Walks in Gower* (Llygad Gwalch Cyf, 2008)
Jenkins, N., *Real Swansea* and *Real Swansea Two* (Seren, 2008 and 2012)
Jennings, C., *The Fast Set* (Little, Brown, 2004)
Lycett, A., *Dylan Thomas: A New Life* (Weidenfeld & Nicolson, 2004)
Richards, A., *Great Walks in Carmarthenshire* (Cwmdwrgi, 2009)
Thomas, D., *Collected Poems* (Dent, 1952)
Thomas, D., *Under Milk Wood* (Dent, 1954)
Tregenna, J., *Buggerall* (Lulu, 2011)

Ordnance Survey maps covering the Tenby to Swansea section of the Wales Coast Path

If you also want to carry large-sized OS Explorer maps, you will need Landranger Nos **158, 177, 178** and **164**; or contact the Ordnance Survey's new Custom Made service at the online shop (www.shop.ordnance surveyleisure.co.uk) to have maps custom-printed to start at Tenby and end at Swansea.

Glossary of Welsh place names

Welsh place names are usually descriptions, some of them quite poetic. But the emphasis is on description.

Many places begin with the word *aber*, meaning the mouth of a river: Aberystwyth, the mouth of the Ystwyth River; Abertawe (the Welsh name for Swansea), the mouth of the Tawe river. Other place names begin with the word *llan*, a church or parish: Llanfair, the

church of (St) Mary; Llanfihangel, the church of (St) Michael.

Plurals in Welsh are usually formed by adding the letters *au* to the end of a word: *dol* (a meadow); *dolau* (meadows).

A small Welsh–English pocket dictionary would be a useful companion in any walker's rucksack. But for the impecunious here is a short glossary of common words and their meanings:

Water

aber estuary	*ffrwd, glais* stream
afon river	*llyn* lake
allt hillside or cliff	*nant* small river, stream
dwr water	*pwll* pool

Land

bre, bryn hill	*cors* bog
bwlch pass	*cwm* valley
cefn ridge, back	*dol* meadow
coed wood	*dyffryn* vale
	glyn glen

gwern marsh
llan enclosed land, parish
maen stone
morfa salt marsh, sea marsh
pen head, end

penrhyn promontory
ystrad dale, valley

Other

bach, fach small
betws chapel
caer, gaer fort
capel chapel

clawdd dyke
croes cross
du black
eglwys church
llys hall, palace
mawr big
melin mill

park park
pont bridge
sir county, shire
tŷ house
tafarn pub
y/yr the
ysbyty hospital

Acknowledgements

I love walking and believe the Wales Coast Path to be a visionary project – let all nations reclaim their coasts and give them back to the boot and the walking pole! As this is an unofficial guide, I had no assistance from the WCP authorities but was helped by many other people. I would like to thank my fellow walkers, especially Kathryn Miller and Jon Tregenna, who also made valuable suggestions for the guide; and also Carolyn Haycock and Gareth Morris; Paul and Andrew at Fairyhill, Gower; Roxanne Treacy of Laugharne; Jane Harris at Visit Wales and Sara Whines at BGB; Eleanor Keatley at the National Wetland Centre; Fiona Reece; Annie Haden at 5 Cwmdonkin Drive; Jo Furber at the Dylan Thomas Centre; Karrimor; Melanie Osborne at the Ordnance Survey; Daniel Dodd at the National Trust; Chris Dale, the ranger on the Swansea/Gower section of the WCP; Chris Delaney of Pendine, who advised on MoD testing in the area; John Pulford, Head of Collections and Interpretation, Brooklands Museum, Weybridge, Surrey; Nigel Jenkins for helpful information on Swansea and Gower; Handshake Group for permission to reproduce lines by Max Boyce on page 87; Quentin Grimley at the Countryside Council for Wales, who clarified statistics on funding; and Alan Kearsley-Evans, head ranger for the National Trust on Gower, who read through that chapter; Brian John, author of the *Pembrokeshire Coast Path National Trail Guide*, whose description of the stretch from Tenby to Amroth formed the basis for my first chapter; Lucy Warburton at Aurum Press for help in compiling the information at the end of each chapter. The photographs were taken by me and by Kathryn Miller, who also did an early edit of the whole text.

A first edition of a brand-new footpath is bound to contain errors – sections of the Wales Coast Path were being built and/or modified even as I walked them – so please drop me a line with any discoveries you make, tips you suggest for a new edition and, of course, any errors or oversights you discover in the text: chris@chris-moss.net.

Useful Information

The Official Guides to all of

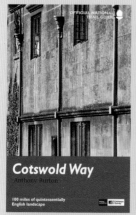

Cotswold Way
Anthony Burton

100 miles of quintessentially
English landscape

ISBN 978 1 84513 785 4

Cleveland Way
Ian Sampson

Over 100 miles of magnificent
walking on the North York Moors

ISBN 978 1 84513 781 6

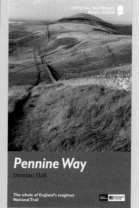

Pennine Way
Damian Hall

The whole of England's toughest
National Trail

ISBN 978 1 84513 718 2

Yorkshire Wolds Way
Roger Ratcliffe

A superbly tranquil walk through
the unspoilt chalk hills of Yorkshire

ISBN 978 178131 064 9

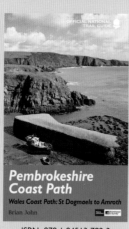

Pembrokeshire Coast Path

Wales Coast Path: St Dogmaels to Amroth
Brian John

ISBN 978 1 84513 782 3

South Downs Way
Paul Millmore

100 miles of glorious chalk downland
for the walker, cyclist and horse rider

ISBN 978 1 78131 088 5

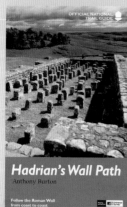

Hadrian's Wall Path
Anthony Burton

Follow the Roman Wall
from coast to coast

ISBN 978 1 84513 808 0

The Ridgeway
Anthony Burton

87 miles of downland walking
from Wiltshire to the Chilterns

ISBN 978 178131 063 2

North Downs Way
Colin Saunders

Follow the chalk ridge across South-East
England all the way to the sea

ISBN 978 178131 061 8